The British Television
Location Guide

Splendid
BOOKS

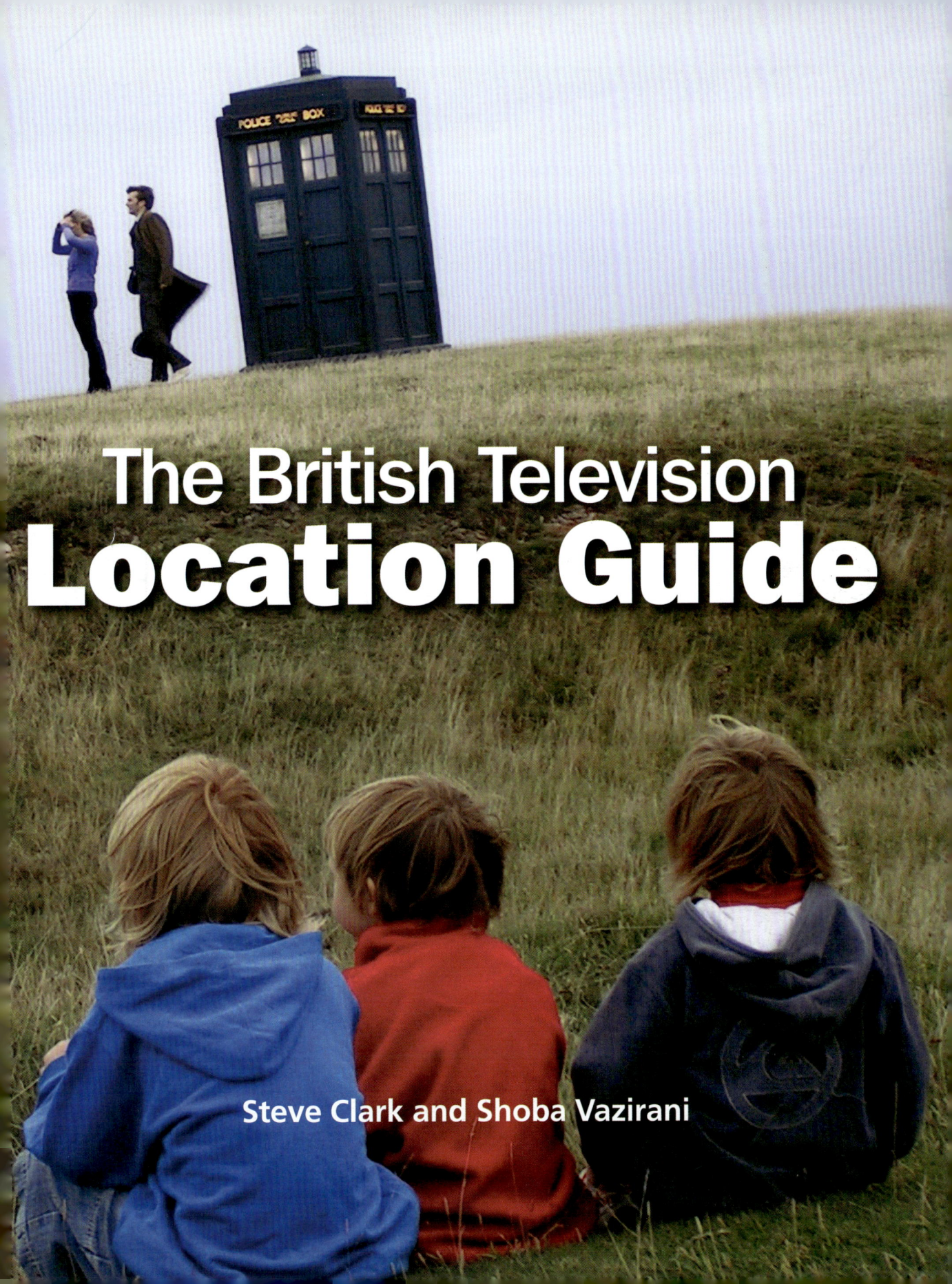

The British Television
Location Guide

Steve Clark and Shoba Vazirani

Contents

For Nicola and Thomas
and for Andy, Imogen, Harry and Abigail

The British Television Location Guide

Written by Steve Clark and Shoba Vazirani

Additional research by Annabel Silk

Copyright © 2011 Splendid Books Limited

The right of Splendid Books Limited to be identified as the Author of the work has been asserted by them in accordance with the Copyright, Designs and Patents Act 1988.

This edition first published in 2011 by Splendid Books Limited

Splendid Books Limited
The Old Hambledon Racecourse Centre
Sheardley Lane
Droxford
Hampshire
SO32 3QY

www.splendidbooks.co.uk

All rights reserved. No part of this publication may be reproduced, stored in a retrieval system, or transmitted in any form including on the Internet or by any means without the written permission of the publisher, nor be otherwise circulated in any form of binding or cover other than that in which it is published and without a similar condition being imposed on the subsequent purchaser.

British Library Cataloguing in Publication Data is available from The British Library

ISBN: 9780955891687

Designed by Design Image Ltd.

www.design-image.co.uk

Printed and bound in Great Britain by Butler, Tanner and Dennis

Every effort has been made to fulfil requirements with regard to reproducing copyright material. The writers and publisher will be glad to rectify any omissions at the earliest opportunity.

Introduction

There can't be many of us who haven't at some point while watching a television series, thought: "I wonder where that was filmed?" Well, hopefully this book will answer many of those questions.

The British Television Location Guide can be enjoyed by those viewers who do their location spotting from their armchairs or by the more adventurous who prefer to go out and visit some of the wonderful places they've seen on screen.

From the splendour of Highclere Castle in Newbury, the setting for wonderful *Downton Abbey,* to the streets of Bristol where many episodes of *Only Fools and Horses* were filmed, the Guide has something for everyone.

Television companies go to great lengths to find perfect locations for their series and often the places they choose aren't well known, so among them are some of the best-kept secrets of the British countryside and its heritage.

While the majority of the locations and places featured in this book are open to the public, there are some that belong to private individuals. We're sure our readers will remember this and respect that these properties are out of bounds.

Obviously lots of the programmes we've covered are filmed in more than one location – often in different parts of the country - but we've listed them in the area where most of the filming took place or, in the case of classic *Doctor Who*, next to a companion section.

Finally, while every effort has been taken to check that all details contained in this book are correct at the time of going to press, readers may wish to confirm directions and opening times before setting out on a long journey.

Happy location hunting!

Steve Clark and Shoba Vazirani

Location Map

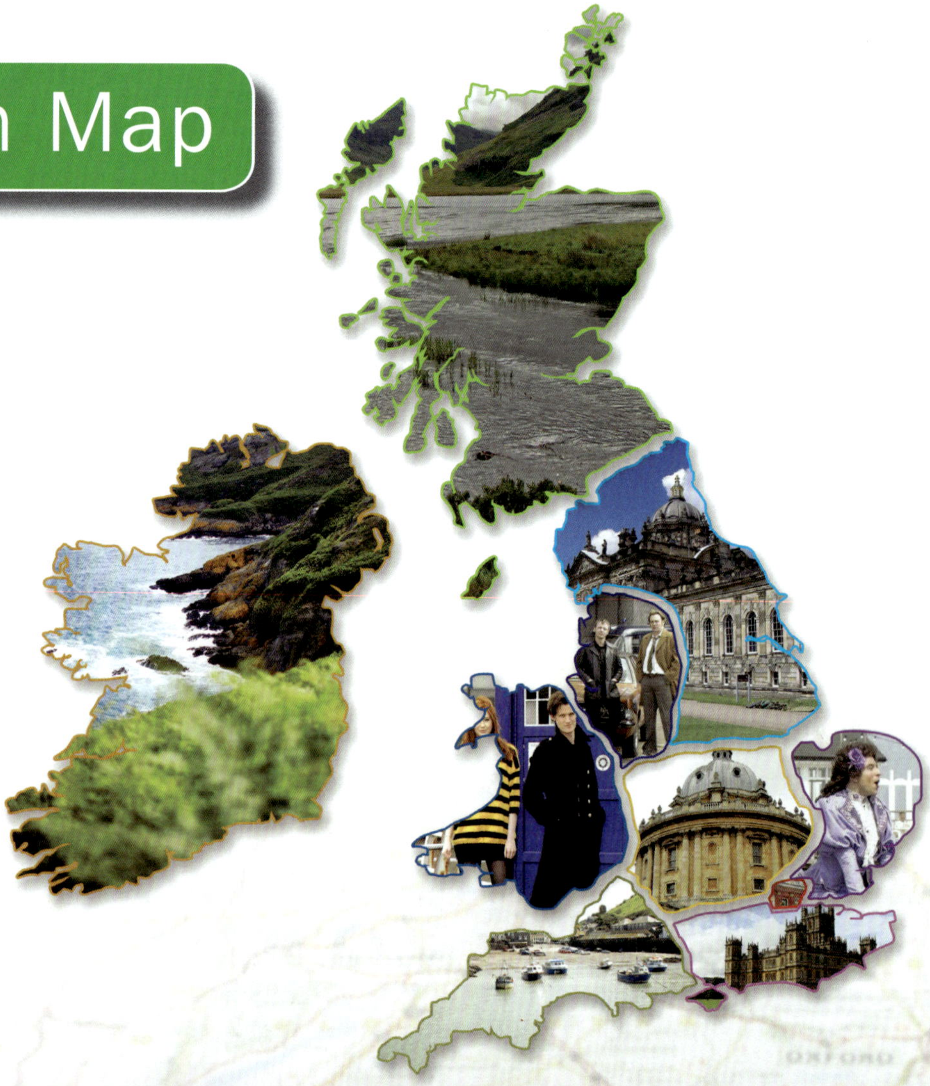

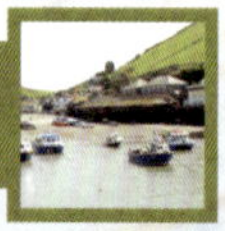
The South West

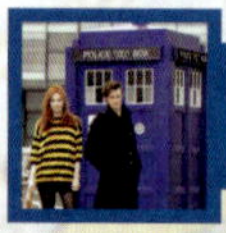
Wales

The South East

The North West

London

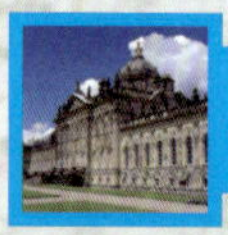
The North

East Anglia

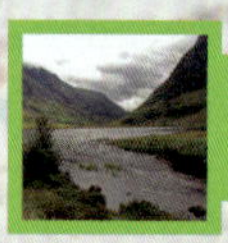
Scotland

The Midlands

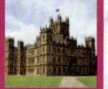

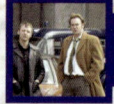

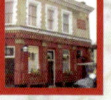

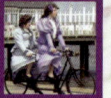

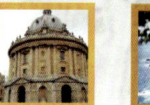

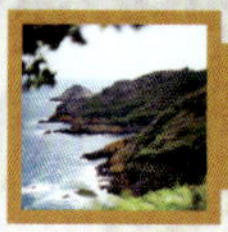
Jersey, Ireland and Northern Ireland

Being Human

Bristol

This supernatural drama about three twenty-something housemates who also happen to be a ghost, a vampire and a werewolf, quickly captured the imagination of a huge audience when the pilot was screened in 2008. The first two series were shot virtually entirely on location in Bristol, a city popular with production companies thanks to its diverse scenery. Fans will easily recognise the famous Clifton Suspension Bridge and can spot scenes filmed in upmarket Clifton Village.

The home of Annie, Mitchell and George is located at Windsor Terrace in Totterdown, an iconic area in the city with multi-coloured houses terraced down some of the steepest hills in the country. A private house was used to shoot exteriors while interiors were filmed on set. The pub the characters are seen drinking in is also located in Windsor Terrace, while Bristol General Hospital was used to film Mitchell and George's place of work and where the romance blossoms between George and Nina. A terrifying scene where Mitchell (Aidan Turner, left) renews his blood-lust is in a hotel room in the Mercure Holland House.

Touchpaper Films which makes the show, was attracted to Bristol's variety of architecture, particularly some of its older buildings which lend a gothic feel, perfect for a drama like *Being Human*. What's more, it was able to take advantage of the city's close proximity to Cardiff where series three was shot and the fourth series will be filmed, as well as the surrounding areas. "Occasionally we needed wilder countryside and as Bristol is near the Mendips we were able to get that easily," said managing director Rob Pursey. The start of series three sees the main characters move to Barry Island in south Wales where they set up home and try and resume their everyday lives. The house used is in Cannon Street, Barry while some filming also took place in the Vale of Glamorgan.

Sat nav references:

Bristol General Hospital (BS1 6SY)

Mercure Holland House (BS1 6SQ)

Bonekickers

Bath

Sat nav references:

Chavenage (GL8 8XP)

Sheldon Manor (SN14 0RG)

Set against the backdrop of the beautiful ancient city of Bath, the 2008 BBC drama *Bonekickers* followed a team of archaeologists as they delved into the past and unravelled ancient mysteries which had relevance to the modern day. They were based at the fictional Wessex University, although the campus of the real-life University of Bath was used for filming as were some rooms in the city's other university, Bath Spa. The historic Roman Baths in Abbey Church Yard featured in several scenes as did the popular famous Assembly Rooms in Bennett Street. Two stately homes made an appearance - Chavenage, just outside Tetbury and Sheldon Manor which is situated at Chippenham, Wiltshire and is one of county's oldest inhabited manor houses. See www.sheldonmanor.co.uk for details.

The Camomile Lawn

Veryan

Fans of the 1992 Channel Four drama *The Camomile Lawn* will be delighted to know that they can actually stay at Broom Parc, the attractive Edwardian clifftop house that was used for the series, as Keith and Lindsay Righton who live there run it as a bed and breakfast.

The house, which was built in 1908 and is actually owned by the National Trust, has wonderful views of the sea but Lindsay said it might not be everyone's ideal home when it gets stormy in the winter. "We're very happy here although other people may not wish to live right on the edge of a cliff in the teeth of a gale and the upkeep of the house is quite substantial. It's very exposed, so if the wind blows the central heating bill goes out of the window!" she added. For more details see www.broomparc.co.uk

Right: **Broom Parc has stunning views of the sea.**

Sat nav reference:
Broom Parc (TR2 5PJ)

Cranford

Lacock

Above: **Turning back the clock - but Lacock didn't need too much work done to make it the perfect place to double as *Cranford*.**

It takes a pretty special television production to entice an Oscar-winning Hollywood actress and that's exactly what the BBC's 2007 dramatisation of the star-studded costume drama *Cranford* proved to be.

Dame Judi Dench thrilled creator Sue Birtwistle when she agreed to take on the role of Miss Matty Jenkyns, whose hopes and rebellious spirit are crushed when she is forced as a young woman to give up the man she loves, played by Michael Gambon. It was the first BBC role for the in-demand actress since she starred in the highly-acclaimed film about Queen Victoria, *Mrs Brown*, ten years earlier.

"It was the quality of the writing and the whole business of it really," she said when asked what pulled her away from the big screen.

The five-part drama, set in a small Cheshire market town in the 1840s, was based on three novels by Elizabeth Gaskell: *Cranford, My Lady Ludlow and Mr Harrison's Confessions* and follows the small absurdities and major tragedies in the lives of the people of *Cranford*. It was so popular that *Cranford* returned for two further episodes screened at Christmas 2009.

Ideally, the production team would have loved to use the town of Knutsford in Cheshire to film *Cranford*. After all, this was Gaskell's original model. But the cost of disguising 21st Century modernisation proved too high and they had to look elsewhere to shoot.

Eventually Lacock in Wiltshire, which has been used for the *Harry Potter* films and dramas including *Pride and Prejudice, Moll Flanders* and *Emma*, was chosen as it is owned by the National Trust and outwardly displays few trappings of modern living. Indeed, visitors to Lacock have remarked how wandering through the stunning village on the southern edge of the Cotswolds is like stepping back into the 18th Century with its stone and thatched cottages and absence of road markings.

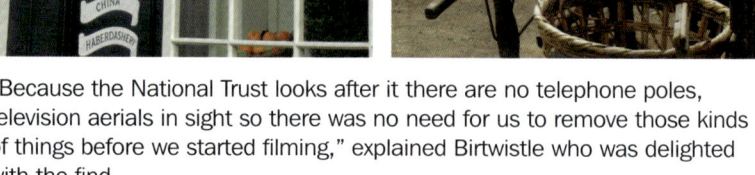

Above: **Dame Judi Dench and Imelda Staunton share a joke during filming** *(centre and right)* **two views of *Cranford* sets where attention to detail was crucial in bringing the series to life.**

"Because the National Trust looks after it there are no telephone poles, television aerials in sight so there was no need for us to remove those kinds of things before we started filming," explained Birtwistle who was delighted with the find.

"We just had to cover the ground [to conceal the tarmac], hide various bits of front doors, redress windows and build the front of Johnson's, *Cranford's* new stores, over the front of the local pub."

The village is within easy reach of Chippenham, Wiltshire by road and rail and boasts Lacock Abbey, a medieval cloistered abbey converted into the splendid country home of William Henry Fox Talbot, who discovered the photographic process, and the Fox Talbot Museum where you can trace the history of photography.

In the centre of the village in the High Street is the 18th Century Red Lion Inn which was perfectly transformed into Johnson's Stores by the BBC where Miss Matty and Miss Deborah Jenkyns (Eileen Atkins) are regularly seen shopping. Assistant Manager Sarah Upton said the conversion of the comfortable Inn into 19th Century 'stores' was impressive and captivated villagers as they watched set designers and engineers construct a whole new 'front' to the building.

"Other streets in the village were also used to double up as the butcher's or dairies and I know some people were asked for use of their homes for various scenes. For about three weeks in April 2007 it was a lot of fun in Lacock!" These days the Red Lion Inn is an idyllic weekend getaway. For reservations telephone 01249 730456.

The National Trust's stunning West Wycombe Park in West Wycombe, Buckinghamshire doubled as Lady Ludlow's home, Hanbury Court. The 18th Century home of Sir Francis Dashwood, founder of the notorious Hellfire Club, it is one of England's finest theatrical houses and with its lavish interiors, complete with fine painted ceilings, it has also proved the perfect setting for other productions, including *Vanity Fair* and *The Importance of Being Earnest*. Telephone 01494 755571 for information about tours.

While making the journey to West Wycombe why not also pop along to the nearby village of Radnage, also within the Chilterns hills and easily accessible from junction 5 of the M40 motorway? Here you'll find the 13th Century-built St Mary's Church which is used in the serial as Cranford Church.

On the edge of the Chiltern Hills is the splendid Ashridge Estate, an area of open countryside and woodland

Above (top): **The ladies of *Cranford* from left to right – Miss Jenkyns (Dame Judi Dench), Miss Dillon (Mary Smith), Miss Pole (Imelda Staunton) and Mrs Forrester (Julia McKenzie)** *(above)* **Philip Glennister as Mr Carter.**

belonging to the National Trust which was used to shoot *Cranford's* May Day scenes, while many of the stunning garden shots were obtained at the Trust's Winkworth Arboretum at Godalming in Surrey. Telephone 01494 755557 for further information on the Ashridge Estate and 01483 208477 for opening arrangements at the Arboretum.

Fans were thrilled when *Cranford* returned to our screens for Christmas 2009. This time the script, again penned by Heidi Thomas, was garnered from a number of Gaskell's stories. Lacock starred as *Cranford* again while West Wycombe Park, Radnage, Syon House and Wasing Park were also revisited.

Anyone wondering where the steam train scenes were filmed may be interested to learn it was actually on the Foxfield Light Railway in Staffordshire, a preserved line originally built in 1893. See www.foxfieldrailway.co.uk for further details.

Sat nav references:

Ashridge Estate (HP4 1LX)

Foxfield Light Railway (ST11 9BG)

Lacock (SN15 2LG)

Red Lion Inn (SN15 2LQ)

St Mary's Church (HP14 4DU)

Syon House (TW7 6AZ)

Wasing Park (RG7 4NG)

Winkworth Arboretum (GU8 4AD)

Doc Martin

Port Isaac

Picturesque Port Isaac on the north Cornwall coast has always been a favourite destination for tourists but now it has extra appeal thanks to the success of ITV's hit drama series *Doc Martin*. The village was originally used as the setting for the 2000 feature film *Saving Grace* which stars Brenda Blethyn as a green-fingered widow who after discovering her late husband has left her with big debts, starts growing marijuana to make money. Martin Clunes co-stars as the local GP.

A year later Sky Pictures decided to make two spin-off films called *Doc Martin* and *Doc Martin and The Legend of The Cloutie* but plans for more films were then put on ice when Sky Pictures shut down in June 2001. But Doc Martin was destined to be seen again and in 2004 filming began on *Doc Martin*, in which the doctor, now called Dr Martin Ellingham, had been a high flying London surgeon but who had to give surgery up after developing a phobia of blood. When the local GP in the sleepy Cornish hamlet of Portwenn, where Ellingham spent his childhood holidays, dies, he

Above: **A view of Port Isaac over the rooftops.**
Opposite page: **Martin Clunes and Caroline Catz pictured during a break in filming in Port Isaac.**

Above: (left) **Doc Martin's house, Fern Cottage** *(centre)* **The Old School House Hotel that is used as Louisa's school and** *(right)* **the narrow streets in the village make driving tricky.**

decides to apply for the job, but the move to the country fails to improve his appalling bedside manner. He doesn't fit in easily as the locals were used to having a friendly GP to talk to and one who would write out a prescription at the drop of a hat. They get a shock when Doctor Ellingham arrives because he couldn't be more curmudgeonly.

"Martin Ellingham might be a clever man in some ways, but he is completely stupid when it comes to dealing with people," said Martin Clunes. "They confound and confuse him. His people skills are terrible and he knows he's like it. He is just useless at small-talk and he's not used to talking to his patients as in his previous job they'd be out cold when he met them ready for him to operate on them."

Port Isaac is a fabulous place and most of the village has been seen in *Doc Martin* at some point. Most notable to location hunters is Fern Cottage - Doc Martin's surgery in the series - up on the left on Roscarrock Hill. The building is clearly visible from pretty much everywhere in Port Isaac, but remember - it is a private house and only the exterior is used for filming (interior scenes are filmed at a studio) and there is a sign in the garden requesting that people do not peer through the windows.

At the bottom of Roscarrock Hill and best viewed from the other side of the harbour, is the stunning waterside house that doubles up as Bert's place. Directly opposite, on the other side of the harbour is the Old School Hotel and Restaurant www.theoldschoolhotel.co.uk the village's former school which is now a hotel but doubles as Portwenn School in the series. It is run by headmistress Louisa Glasson (Caroline Catz) whose will-they, won't-they relationship with the Doctor keeps viewers intrigued. Nearby is the Boathouse Stores which has appeared in the show and a few doors up from the hotel is Louisa's cottage.

The roads in Port Isaac are very narrow and you might want to consider parking at the top of the hill and walking down to the harbour. If you do decide to venture down by car then, if the tide is out, you can park on the beach – but keep an eye on the water level! There are plenty of decent places to eat with everything from a cup of tea to a full culinary experience on offer. Among the places to eat is The Golden Lion pub, which doubles as The Crab and Lobster in *Doc Martin*, and nearby, in Middle Street, is the building that doubles as the chemist shop. Telephone the Golden Lion Pub on 01208 880336.

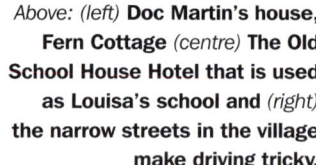

Sat nav references:

Boathouse Stores (PL29 3RA)

Golden Lion pub (PL29 3RB)

Old School Hotel and Restaurant (PL29 3RD)

Harbour Lights
West Bay

Set in the small Dorset village of West Bay, BBC drama *Harbour Lights* was expected to be a roaring success when it hit our screens in 1999 due to its star, *Heartbeat's* Nick Berry. Sadly, despite the pretty setting, it failed to impress viewers and was axed after two series. Berry played harbourmaster Mike Nicholl, an ex-Royal Navy Lieutenant Commander now in charge of the harbour of a small south coast town called Bridehaven where feuding families, ruthless business dealings and the sea dominated the lives of the people who work and play there.

The quaint real-life 16th Century Bridport Arms Hotel, close to the sea, was one of the show's key locations and actually played two different places in the series. It offers accommodation - see: www.bridportarms.co.uk for details. The BBC built a false porch on the landlord's bottle store outside the hotel, changed the door and hey presto, it became Nicholl's fictional home. Nearby is the Harbour Café which on screen was run by music-loving Elvis. The on-screen harbourmaster's office was over the other side of the harbour and the exterior was used for filming although interior scenes were usually shot elsewhere to avoid disrupting the work of the real harbourmaster.

Sat nav references:

Bridport Arms Hotel (DT6 4EN)

Harbour Café (DT6 4ER)

The House of Eliott
West Bay

Modern day Bristol played 1920s London for the BBC's drama *The House of Eliott*. The city was chosen to double as the capital because it was easier and cheaper to film outside London and the houses in parts of Bristol fitted the bill. The exterior of Beatrice and Evangeline's (Stella Gonet and Louise Lombard, pictured left) House of Eliott design studio was filmed at number 24 Berkeley Square. When the BBC arrived they had to remove all traces of the 1990s to recreate London of the 1920s.

Yellow lines were covered up with either latex paint or special mats which looked like cobblestones and the tops of parking meters were removed. Modern intercom systems on the outside of many of the buildings were usually disguised as old-fashioned doorplates. The Bristol branch of Coutts, in Corn Street, was used as fictional Gillespie Saroyan Bank and Clifton Girls School played home to Jack's apartment. The Wills Memorial Building at Bristol University also played the interior of the Houses of Parliament and the former Will's Cigarette Factory was used as Jack's film studio. Royal Fort House in Royal Fort Gardens played the offices of a rival fashion house, Hauseurs. Clifton Hill House, a university hall of residence, was used for a dinner party scene and the Orangery at another hall of residence, Goldney House doubled as a teashop. Just across the River Avon at Leigh Woods is Leigh Court a former mental hospital, which was used on the programme to play the interior of the Houses of Parliament, the interior of Buckingham Palace and the foyer of the Ritz Hotel.

Lark Rise to Candleford

Tetbury

Above: **The amazing set the BBC built for the filming of *Lark Rise to Candleford*.**

The first series of this charming and heart-warming drama was shot in 2007 and screened by the BBC the following year, much to the delight of Sunday evening viewers. Flora Thompson's autobiographical novel *Lark Rise to Candleford* was beautifully adapted by Bill Gallagher and won critical acclaim for its stunning depiction of the English countryside.

Sadly, despite impressive viewer ratings, the BBC decided the fourth series of *Lark Rise to Candleford* was to be the last and the drama bowed out on February 13 2011, leaving fans wishing there could be more.
The drama was set in Lark Rise, a small Oxfordshire hamlet and the neighbouring market town of Candleford and examined the lives of workers and gentry as the 19th Century drew to a close.

Their everyday comings and goings and concerns were seen through the eyes of Laura Timmins, played by actress Olivia Hallinan, who, when the story began, moved from Lark Rise to the wealthier Candleford to begin a new life, to work for her mother's cousin Dorcas (Julia Sawalha) at the local post office.

Above: **Beautiful Chavenage, one of the main locations for *Lark Rise to Candleford.***

Although set in Oxfordshire, *Lark Rise* (which also starred Dawn French in series one, two and four and Claudie Blakley), was actually filmed in and around Gloucestershire and Wiltshire, both at specially built studios and more prominently, at the stunning Chavenage House which played Sir Timothy Midwinter's home Candleford Manor.

Both interiors and exteriors of the Manor were shot extensively at Chavenage which is just outside the market town of Tetbury, not far from Prince Charles' home Highgrove, taking full advantage of its beautiful gardens outside and inside, its oak-floored, exquisitely decorated rooms which are steeped in history.

Originally built in 1383, there have been additions and renovations to the property over the centuries. Since Tudor times only two families have owned Chavenage, the current owner David Lowsley-Williams having inherited the House from his uncle John in 1958.

These days, the property is very much a family home and even though it is open to the public on a part-time basis and incidentally, the perfect wedding venue, members of the Lowsley-Williams clan are never far away. David and his wife Rona have three children – George, Caroline and Joanna - and six grandchildren who enjoy running around the 1400-acre estate with their dogs and riding their ponies.

Caroline organises weddings – bookings have already been taken for years ahead - corporate events and of course filming and she says the family were delighted when the BBC approached them to shoot Lark Rise at their home.

While it wasn't the first time Chavenage was used as a film location – an episode of ITV's *Poirot* was shot there as was part of the 2008 BBC series *Bonekickers* and an episode of *Casualty* – it was the first time the house was featured so heavily in a major television drama.

"The location manager's brief was to find unspoiled countryside close to a manor house which was a difficult search," explained Caroline. "I showed her round Chavenage and although she'd been here before, it was as though a light bulb went on in her head."

Not only is the house made of limestone which is in keeping with the description of Candleford Manor, but do a 360 degree turn outside and nothing that wasn't there before 1881 such as electricity pylons and telephone cables, comes into view. Perfect.

Filming began in the early summer of 2007 but a particularly rainy season meant that certain scenes had to be shot again two or three months later. For instance, an area of picturesque garden set for a relaxing picnic turned into a lake as storms battered the south west. Also, an outbreak of foot and mouth disease meant that no pigs were available for the farm scenes.

Fans of *Lark Rise to Candleford* will recognise many of the rooms used if they visit Chavenage such as the panelled Oak Room which doubled up as Lady Adelaide's drawing room, what the family call the Ante Room, which served as Sir Timothy's office and the Ball Room which was the dining room in the series.

The Great Hall was also frequently on display as the hall at Candleford Manor and where characters were often seen passing through to the outside, which was also filmed extensively. As to be expected, the BBC asked to make certain alterations to the premises before shooting could commence and the Lowsley-Williams agreed.

"A big change was the gravel on the driveway which was blue granite originally but had to be limestone for the BBC's use," Caroline revealed. "So they had our gravel taken out and theirs put in which has stayed since.

"There are security lights outside the house which had to be covered up for filming purposes but they had to be uncovered every night for insurance reasons. So they made little polystyrene 'hats' which could go on and off easily.

"Also, they gave us two standard lamps. Some of the lights in one of the rooms had to be removed and covered up with panelling because obviously the series is set in pre-electric times. So they kindly gave us the lamps instead."

If you're wondering where most of the village scenes were shot, these were at a Grade II listed farm at Box, five miles east of Bath where a temporary village was specially created. Nearby Neston Park in Corsham with its beautiful historical buildings is also used as a backdrop for much of all four series with many scenes shot on location in a farmyard, while a vast warehouse in Yate, 12 miles north east of Bristol was transformed into no fewer than 16 sets of many of the village and town interior scenes.
For further details about Chavenage House telephone 01666 502329 or see www.chavenage.com

Above top: **Dawn French with some young friends at Chavenage, one of the main locations for *Lark Rise to Candleford*.** *Above:* **Olivia Grant, who plays Lady Adelaide Midwinter, pictured during a break in filming.**

Sat nav references

Chavenage House (GL8 8XP)
Neston Park (SN13 9TG)

Mistresses

Bristol

The tangled love lives of four 30-something modern women, all glamorous and successful in their own right, made Ecosse Films' drama for the BBC, *Mistresses*, unmissable week-night television when it was first screened in January 2008. Sadly, for many viewers, the show starring Sarah Parish, Sharon Small, Orla Brady, Shelley Conn and Joanna Lumley in the final series, was axed after season three in August 2010.

While the glossy drama could have been filmed anywhere, it was actually the more glamorous locations of Bristol that were selected and help to give *Mistresses* a sophisticated feel. Bristol University doubled up as a restaurant in one episode and the General Medical Council in another, filming taking place after students left in the summer of 2007. The big finale sequence in series one took place in At Bristol, a hands-on science tourist attraction at trendy Millennium Square in the centre of the city.

Real restaurants and hotels used in *Mistresses* included Bordeaux Quay on Canons Road, The Olive Shed at Princes Wharf and The Riverstation Restaurant www.riverstation.co.uk Other places of interest featured include the historic Blaise Castle Estate which boasts a small gothic castle dating back to the 18th Century called the Folly. The Folly is now a ruin and is open to the public on certain days during the summer only. For more information contact the Estate Office on 0117 353 2268.

Sat nav references:

Blaise Castle Estate (BS10 7QS)

Bordeaux Quay (BS1 5LL)

Olive Shed at Princes Wharf (BS1 4RN)

The Onedin Line

Dartmouth

Anyone who visited the pretty town of Dartmouth in Devon during certain periods of the 1970s must have thought they had walked through a time tunnel. For the clock was turned back on much of the town and surrounding areas while the BBC filmed its popular period drama *The Onedin Line*. The drama, which was set in the 1860s, followed the life of James Onedin, played by Peter Gilmore, as he ran his shipping line.

Right: **Bayard's Cove in Dartmouth, a key location for *The Onedin Line*.**

Sat nav references:

The Dartmouth Arms (TQ6 9AN)

George and Dragon (TQ6 9NG)

Maltster's Arms (TQ9 7EH)

Historic Bayard's Cove, which includes the Old Customs House and The Dartmouth Arms, was featured in several episodes. Nearby Bayard's Cove Fort was used for a Middle Eastern market scene as was the outside of the George and Dragon in Mayors Avenue and a scene supposedly in China was filmed in Avenue Gardens.

One Foot in the Grave

Christchurch

There were probably real cries of "I Don't Believe It" in sleepy Tresillian Way, a small street in the village of Walkford near Christchurch in Dorset during the 1990s. For, as the real life setting for David Renwick's hit comedy series *One Foot in the Grave*, some very strange things happened. Like 263 garden gnomes being delivered to the front lawn of poor old Victor Meldrew or an old Citroen being dumped in his skip. Life for Victor (Richard Wilson) was rather testing a lot of the time and that in turn didn't make things very easy for his long-suffering wife Margaret.

Below: (left) **Tresillian Way, Walkford** *(centre)* **tributes to Victor** *(right)* **Victor and Margaret.**

The series ran from 1990 until 2000 and when Victor finally ended up in a grave after falling victim to a hit and run driver, fans made sure he wasn't forgotten. In fact floral tributes were laid near a railway bridge at Shawford near Winchester near to the spot where Victor met his end. Richard Wilson told the local paper, the Hampshire Chronicle, that Shawford was "the perfect place" for Victor to end his days. "I can't give anything away," he said. "But I can see why we've come here. It's very picturesque."

Only Fools and Horses

Bristol

It's no real wonder that the long arm of the law has never quite managed to catch up with dodgy dealing Del Boy Trotter. For if the boys in blue have been looking for Del in his manor of Peckham they've been looking in the wrong place. John Sullivan's brilliant *Only Fools And Horses* – which starred David Jason as wheeler-dealer Del Boy Trotter and Nicholas Lyndhurst as his dopey brother Rodney – became increasingly rarely shot in London - and has never actually been shot in Peckham. It used to be filmed in and around the capital until it became too popular on screen and the crowds who gathered to watch filming grew too large. "Filming in London was a pain in the neck and we used to lose a lot of filming," said Ray Butt, the show's first producer. "I remember filming in Chapel Street in London and the crowds used to come round but they wouldn't be quiet and usually we'd have to stop during school breaks. It just became impossible to work."

Above top: **David Jason and Nicholas Lyndhurst share a joke during the filming of** *Only Fools and Horses*
Above: **David Jason and Nicholas Lyndhurst take a break while filming** *Only Fools and Horses* **outside.**

Originally lots of London locations were used including Hammersmith cemetery, where Granddad's funeral took place, in *Strained Relations*, The Alma pub at the corner of Chapel Market and Baron Street in Islington which was seen in *It Never Rains* and *Diamonds Are For Heather* and Hanwell Community Centre Westcott Crescent, London, which was in *Cash and Curry*. Witley Gardens, Southall Green, was the street in *Ashes to Ashes*, where Trigger's grandfather's urn was sucked up by a passing road sweeper lorry and Ravenscourt Park in Hammersmith in the episode *As One Door Closes*. Outside London, Butser Hill, near Petersfield, Hampshire was used for the hang gliding scene in *Tea For Three* and the Duke of Malebury's stately home in *A Royal Flush* was Clarendon Park, Wiltshire, but it isn't open to the public.

The series began to be filmed all round the country and there was a Nag's Head in Hull, Ipswich, Brighton, London and Bristol and a Peckham street market in Hull, Ipswich, Bristol and Salisbury. As Ray Butt said: "You can set up a street market anywhere. All you need is a long run of walls and then put some stalls out." Bristol though became the most regularly used setting for the show. "Architecturally it had everything we needed in terms of pubs, houses and a market and most importantly we found the right block of flats," said producer Gareth Gwenlan. So instead of Harlech Tower, Park Road East, Acton, London, the original setting, Whitemead House in Duckmoor Road, Bristol became Nelson Mandela House for the duration of filming and residents got used to seeing Del's dodgy yellow three-wheeler parked nearby.

From then on, many parts of Bristol were used for filming the show including: In *Dates*, Bristol North Baths, Gloucester Road, which was the police station, 46 Old Market Street, which was the dating agency, and The White Horse, West Street, Bedminster, which was the Nag's Head. 187 Gloucester Road, now Planet Pizza, is where Trigger took a date and Shellard Road in Filton was where Rodney jumped a red light while trying to impress nervous Nerys. London also features briefly - the Trotter van flying over a bridge was shot at Talbot Road, Isleworth and Del and Raquel met under the clock at Waterloo Station. The Old Granary, Charlotte Street, which appears in *Yuppy Love*, where it served as the exterior location of the basement wine bar where Del famously fell over and also played a casino in *Fatal Extraction*, is now a Loch Fyne restaurant. Across the road at 46-48 Charles Fox House was the location of Rodney's adult education class. The Parkside Night Club, Bath Road, 10-16 York Street (which was used as Alan Parry's business), flats at Guild Court, Redcliffe Back and the Boardwalk Shopping Centre were all used in *Rodney Come Home*. Henry Africas Hothouse, Whiteladies Road and Shoots floating restaurant were both used for *The Chance of a Lunchtime* and Raquel's audition in *Stage Fright* took place at the Courage Social Club in Willway Road.

The Conservatory Bar at Arnos Manor Hotel on Bath Road in Bristol was used in *Danger UXD* in the scene where Rodney took Cassandra to dinner. The hotel was also the venue for disco scenes in *Yuppy Love* and *Rodney Come Home*. The rear of Arnos Manor Hotel in Bath Road was used in *Chain Gang* as the One Eleven Club. Lockside Cafe on Brunel Lock Road, Bristol was the location for Sid's Cafe in the 1993 Xmas Special *Fatal Extraction* and the 1996 episodes *Heroes and Villains* and *Modern Men*. Back then it was a greasy spoon, but

Above: **Whitemead House**
Right: **Del and Rodney do a runner.**

now, according to its website www.lockside.net, it is a 'polished spoon.' A car showroom on Marsh Road was the location for Boycie's car showroom in *Time on our Hands* and Bristol City's car park at Ashton Gate was used as a market in *Fatal Extraction*, *Heroes and Villains*, and *Strangers on the Shore*. But Bristol didn't have a monopoly on filming. For example, the former Bembom Brothers' funfair at Margate (now called Dreamland), the Roman Galley pub in Thanet Way, Canterbury (which has now been converted into flats called Galley View) and the forecourt of Margate railway station were all used for the episode *The Jolly Boys' Outing* and *Tandoori Nights*, King Street, London appeared in *Chain Gang*. It was also back to London for scenes of Del and Rodney searching for Albert in *He Ain't Heavy, He's My Uncle* and the following places were used: Tower Bridge, HMS Belfast, Portobello Green, Acklam Road East, Malton Road and Portobello Road Market. The airport used in *The Sky's The Limit* was Stansted.

The hilarious scene when Raquel gave birth to Damian Trotter was supposed to be in Peckham but was actually filmed at the maternity wing of Hillingdon Hospital in Uxbridge in the episode *Three Men, a Woman and a Baby*. The scenes of Damian's christening in *Miami Twice: The American Dream* were actually filmed at two different churches. The interior scenes were filmed at St John's Church in Ladbroke Grove and the outside shots were done at St John's Church in Kentish Town. The Nag's Head used for the 1992 Christmas special *Mother Nature's Son* was the White Admiral Pub at Lower Bevendean in Brighton (sadly now demolished with flats now built on the site) not far from the allotments in Natal Road which were used as Grandad's old allotment in Peckham.

The area in front of Whitemead House, Bristol, was used for the riot scene in *Fatal Extraction*. It was back to Bristol for the famous Batman and Robin scene in *Heroes and Villains* which was filmed at the shopping centre at The Horsefair in Broadmead and Rodney chases a yob past shops in Oxford Street and also down Nottingham Street and Hill Avenue in the same episode. The Harrison watch was found at Del's garage, a stone's throw from Whitemead House and when the Trotters sell it in *Time on Our Hands*, the auction scenes were filmed at Sotheby's, 34-35 New Bond Street, London. Marine Parade, Woodland Road, and the Dragon Kiss restaurant in Regent Street, Weston-Super-Mare all appear in *If They Could See Us Now* and if you fancy a trip abroad, Del and Rodney took a ferry from Portsmouth to represent Albert at a ceremony in France, scenes for which were filmed in Gatteville-le-Phare. Finally, in the last episode *Sleepless in Peckham*, Greenbank Cemetery in Greenbank Road, Bristol was used for a moving scene where Rodney and Del visit their Mum's grave.

Persuasion

Bath

Beautiful and historical Bath featured heavily in ITV's stunning adaptation of Jane Austen's *Persuasion* which was filmed in 2006 and screened the following year to critical acclaim. It's a city close to Jane Austen's heart as she lived there in the early 1800s and chose it as the setting for both *Northanger Abbey* and *Persuasion*. This version starred Rupert Penry-Jones as Captain Wentworth and Sally Hawkins as Anne Elliot, an 'old maid' of 27 living a quiet life with her noble family in their country manor home, Kellynch Hall until events force a change on the whole family, particularly Anne. "We tried to base as much of *Persuasion* as we could in Bath but there were some locations we had to travel outside the city for," explained Location Manager Fiona Francombe. "But even then, we tried to stay as close to the area as we could. We filmed beach scenes at Lyme Regis in Dorset on the Cobb which was great. We also filmed at Golden Cap, five miles east of Lyme Regis."

Stunning Sheldon Manor in Chippenham doubled as Uppercross Hall to where Anne decamps after her family are forced to leave Kellynch. One of the oldest inhabited manor houses in Wiltshire with sections dating back to the 13th Century, the property boasts glorious gardens making it an idyllic wedding – and of course filming – location. The house is open to the public and can be hired out for special functions. See www.sheldonmanor.co.uk for details. The Coaching Inn which, supposedly at Lyme Regis, was actually shot at Great Chalfield Manor, near Melksham in Wiltshire. Chalfield is looked after by the National Trust and is renowned for its gardens. Indeed these were filmed extensively for scenes of Anne and her cousins out walking. Telephone 01225 782239 to find out about opening times or see

Below: **Bath Street in Bath - used for a market scene in ITV's 2006 version of *Persuasion*.**

Above: **Rupert Penry-Jones and Sally Hawkins pictured during a break in the filming of *Persuasion*.**

www.nationaltrust.org.uk The interior of Camden Place, the Bath property the Elliott family head to after leasing out Kellynch, was actually Neston Park in Corsham and the exterior was Number One Royal Crescent in the centre of Bath. Neston Park is a country estate owned by the Fuller family (as in Fuller's London Pride ale), built in 1790. In case you were wondering, the elegant and stately Kellynch itself was filmed at a private house, the owners of which prefer not to make public. The National Trust-owned Assembly Rooms in Bennett Street were used to stage a concert during which Captain Wentworth sees Anne and leaves. The rooms are home to the Fashion Museum and are available to hire for special events. Go to www.nationaltrust.org.uk to find out more. Bennett Street itself was also used as the address of Mrs Smith and Westgate Buildings. It also doubled as Queens Square, which itself was too small to close down for filming purposes. Royal Crescent doubled as Camden Place to where Anne's father and sister moved when they leave Kellynch and the romantic final scene where Anne and Wentworth kiss at the end of *Persuasion* was also shot there.

The beautiful Botanical Gardens in Royal Victoria Park became the exterior of Queens Square which again was unsuitable for filming on that particular day. Nearby Western Road was closed during shooting to minimise noise. The very narrow cobbled Queen Street was used on another day for a scene in which Wentworth is searching for Anne. He looks in an art shop window and so a shop was specially dressed for the purpose. The final day of filming took place at Green Park where Anne and Wentworth finally admit their feelings to each other. Grand Parade was also used for one of these closing scenes, along with Bath Street. The latter was transformed into a spectacular period market which was all the more amazing considering it is one of the busiest streets in the city centre, being as it is in close proximity to the ever popular Roman Baths.

The 1995 version of *Persuasion* was arguably the BBC's finest adaptation of a Jane Austen novel by virtue of Director Roger Michell's deliberately dowdy costumes and settings, making it altogether less glossy than other Austen dramatisations. Much was filmed in Bath with both the Assembly Rooms and Pump Room being used for some scenes including a concert. The nearby Abbey Churchyard also featured as did 13 Old Bond Street, now a Starbucks coffee shop, which played a teashop. A private house at 94 Sydney Place was used as several different screen settings. Outside Bath beautiful Sheldon Manor at Chippenham, the surviving manor house of a long gone Medieval village, also appeared in this version doubling as The Musgrove's home. Barnsley House at Barnsley near Cirencester in Gloucestershire played Kellynch Hall in *Persuasion* and is now a hotel and wedding venue. See www.barnsleyhouse.com for details.

Sat nav references:

Assembly Rooms (BA1 2QH)

Barnsley House (GL7 5EE),

Great Chalfield Manor (SN12 8NH)

Neston Park in Corsham (SN13 9TG)

Number One Royal Crescent (BA1 2LR)

Sheldon Manor (SN14 0RG)

Poldark

Cornwall

Cornwall was the setting for *Poldark*, the BBC's swashbuckling saga about heroic war veteran Ross Poldark, played by Robin Ellis. Set in the 18th Century the series was a huge hit with viewers both in Britain and around the world, who revelled in the stories of tin mining, smuggling and skulduggery. Ross and his wife Demelza, played by Angharad Rees lived at Nampara, which is actually a stone farmhouse, Botallack Manor. Other scenes at Nampara were filmed at nearby Pendeen Manor. Ross' cousin Francis and his wife Elizabeth, live at Trenwith. In the first series Trenwith was played by Tudor Godolphin House at Godolphin Cross. Godolphin, which is now owned by the National Trust, was used when Trenwith is sacked and burnt, when Trenwith is attacked by miners and scenes where Ross Poldark first meets Demelza at the Redruth Fair were filmed in the grounds.

Dr Dwight Enys' home in the series was actually Doyden Castle, a gothic folly built in the 19th Century. The folly, at Port Quin in north Cornwall, is high up on the cliffs and has spectacular views. It can be rented from the National Trust. Not far from Port Quin, at Trebetherick, is Enodoc Church which was used for the wedding of Francis and Elizabeth. Another church, Towednack, was used for Francis' father's funeral. Lots of filming took place on the north coast from Botallack in the far west to the River Camel where Padstow stands, in the Penzance area, Prussia Cove, and on the south coast at Charlestown, which was also used for the 1998 ITV drama Frenchman's Creek. Cornwall also doubled for France with part of the Fowey estuary, near Lerryn Creek playing a landing point for Ross and his friends in their bid to free Dr Enys from French prison Fort Baton. St Mawes Castle, an English Heritage property, at the entrance to Falmouth played the fort. See www.english-heritage.org.uk for further details.

Right: **Stunning St Mawes Castle in Falmouth, doubled as a French fort in *Poldark*.**

Sat nav references:

Botallack Manor (TR19 7QG)

Enodoc Church (PL27 6SA)

Pendeen Manor (TR19 7ED)

St Mawes Castle (TR2 5DE)

Tudor Godolphin House (TR13 9RE)

Sense and Sensibility

Bideford

Anyone familiar with the stunning coastal walkway between Hartland Quay and Hartland Point which is to be found on the Hartland Abbey Estate near Bideford, north Devon may well have recognised it while watching the BBC's superb adaptation of Jane Austen's *Sense and Sensibility*. It was here that much of the three-part serialisation starring such names as David Morrissey and Janet McTeer was filmed during an often wet May 2007. The Estate, which has been classified as an area of outstanding natural beauty, is owned by Sir Hugh and Lady Angela Stucley and tucked away in a sheltered valley is Blackpool Mill Cottage which was heavily featured in the drama, as Barton Cottage.

It was to here that the Dashwood Family – sisters Elinor (Hattie Morahan) and Marianne (Charity Wakefield) - decamp upon the death of their father, along with their widowed mother (McTeer) and begin to build themselves a new life. But the cottage seen in the drama looks somewhat different to the actual building used thanks to the skills of the BBC's set designers, as Lady Stucley explained: "They added dormer windows to the roof of the cottage, shutters and a porch which actually didn't go anywhere. The actors were seen stepping inside but it was just a front. They also added a chimney to the sea end of the property so they had three chimneys instead of the two that are normally there."

The BBC also obtained the family's permission to paint the cottage and then returned it to its natural state once filming was over. If you fancy staying at Blackpool Mill cottage, it is available for rent for up to eight people. See www.hartlandabbey.com for details.

The Stucleys themselves live in Hartland Abbey which has been in their family since it was handed to them by Henry VIII. A stunning building, it is the obvious choice for many a location manager as are the five miles of coastline which belongs to the family. "We're used to having camera crews filming in our

Right: **Picturesque Blackpool Mill Cottage used as Barton Cottage in** *Sense and Sensibility.*

Above: **Loseley House, a key location for *Sense and Sensibility*.**

midst," Lady Stucley continued. "The grounds of Hartland Abbey were used as a production base for *Sense and Sensibility* and it was great fun having actors wandering about in costumes eating ice-creams and mingling with everyone." In fact, in some scenes part of the grounds of the Abbey were used as the carriageway for other stately homes the BBC filmed at.

These include Dorney Court in Windsor, Berkshire which served as the grand home of Sir John Middleton (played by Mark Williams). It was here that a lavish dinner party scene took place as did the rehearsal for a ball the Dashwood sisters attend. Privately owned, it is a Grade I listed building of outstanding historical interest. See www.dorneycourt.co.uk for further details.

The sumptuous 17th Century Ham House on the banks of the River Thames at Ham, Richmond-Upon-Thames doubled up as Cleveland. The house, which belongs to the National Trust, has stunning formal gardens which have been partially restored, as well as gorgeous interiors and original collections. See www.national-trust.org.uk for information about visiting times. The spectacular Dyrham House, a William and Mary mansion set in a deer park, also belonging to the Trust was used to shoot many of the garden scenes. The location can also be glimpsed in the movie *Remains of the Day* shot in 1993. Finally, the splendid library at historic Loseley Park just outside Guildford, Surrey which is a stunning wedding venue for many a lucky bride, played Colonel Brandon's library. The front entrance of Loseley was also used in *Sense and Sensibility* for the scenes in which Colonel Brandon and his guests, including the Dashwoods, gather in preparation for his picnic which doesn't happen as he is called away on urgent business. The House also doubled as the exterior of Sir John's home which, of course, is set in Devon in the story, while its impressive Oak Room was used in the series to nurse a sick Marianne after her walk in the rain. See www. loseley-park.com for more information.

Sat nav references:

Blackpool Mill Cottage (EX39 6DT)

Dorney Court (SL4 6QP)

Dyrham House (SN14 8ER)

Ham House (TW10 7RS)

Hartland Abbey Estate (EX39 6DT)

Loseley Park (GU3 1HS)

Skins

Bristol

Teen drama *Skins* began airing on E4 then Channel 4 in 2007 and has proved to be a huge hit, particularly with youngsters who can identify with its modern-day issues such as relationship angst, infidelity, drugs and pressures of school. Focusing on a group of Bristol teenagers, the city itself features heavily throughout most episodes of all series shot so far and a number of Bristol landmarks are readily recognisable such as Bristol Cathedral which is shown in the opening credits of series one and the Pur Down BT transmission tower situated to the right of the M32 as you enter Bristol, with wonderful views over the city in the opening credits of series two.

The unit base for *Skins* is in a large warehouse in Fishponds, north Bristol. "They base themselves there then build sets there for house and club interiors," explained Natalie Moore, formerly of Bristol Film Office. "For exteriors they use Brandon Hill quite a lot." Brandon Hill is one of the city's oldest public parks, gifted to the council in 1147 by the Earl of Gloucester and boasting spectacular views across Bristol. For details of opening times contact Bristol Parks on 0117 922 3719.

Other parks and council-owned estates around Bristol used for filming include The Kings Weston Estate, Oldbury Court Estate, Ashton Court Estate and Queens Square. For series one many college scenes were shot at The John Cabot Academy, an independent school in Kingswood, north east Bristol. For series two the production team decided to recreate the headmaster's office and a classroom on a studio set and so used the Academy a lot less.

About 200 yards from Brandon Hill is College Green which is at the bottom of Park Street, outside the council offices. It is here that the teens in *Skins* often congregate after class and it is a regular feature. On screen it is supposedly right outside the college when actually it is filmed in a totally different location. *Skins'* Location Manager David Johnson said: "Other places of interest to visitors are Thekla which is a cool boat that sits on the side of Bristol Harbour and where the characters had a big party in series three." Go to www.theklabristol.co.uk for more details. Nightclubs used in *Skins* include Lakota, La Rocca and The Croft which are popular and well-known while David recommends tourists visit St Nicholas's Market in Central Bristol and Cabot Circus, a large and impressive shopping centre.

The main Bristol University building often doubled up for several different venues in early seasons of *Skins* while the once-derelict Pro-Cathedral was used as the venue for a huge 'secret party' in season two which was filmed exclusively for the internet and to which 500 fans of the show were invited. The building has since been redeveloped.

Sat nav references:

Ashton Court Estate (BS41 9DW)

Brandon Hill (BS1 5RR)

Bristol Cathedral (BS1 5TJ)

The Croft (BS1 3RW)

John Cabot Academy (BS15 8BD)

The Kings Weston Estate (BS11 0UR)

Lakota (BS2 8QE)

La Rocca (BS8 1EY)

Oldbury Court Estate (BS16 2QX)

To the Manor Born

Cricket St Thomas

Above: (left) **Filming To the Manor Born at night** *(centre)* **Cricket St Thomas, alias Grantleigh Manor** *(right)* **the famous clapperboard.**
Right: **Penelope Keith and Peter Bowles filming the 2007 Christmas special.**

The BBC had a winner on its hands in 1979 with its comedy series *To the Manor Born.* The show starred Penelope Keith as frightfully posh Audrey Fforbes-Hamilton who, stung by death duties, was forced to sell her stately home, Grantleigh Manor, and live in the estate's tiny lodge, taking her butler Brabinger and her beagle Benjie with her.

Grantleigh Manor was bought by self-made millionaire grocer Richard De Vere who, certainly in the eyes of Mrs Fforbes-Hamilton, doesn't come from the right kind of background necessary to live in such a place. But he obviously grew on her, as they married at the end of the series and are still together in a special episode shown at Christmas 2007.

The series was filmed on the elegant Cricket St Thomas estate, near Chard in Somerset. Cricket House naturally plays Grantleigh Manor and the estate's lodge plays Mrs Fforbes-Hamilton's modest residence.

The estate was bought in 1998 by Warner Leisure Hotels and the house, which was built in 1785 and is Grade II listed, has been turned into a resort hotel offering four-star accommodation. For details of how to book accommodation at Cricket St Thomas see www.warnerleisurehotels.co.uk

Sat nav reference:

Cricket St Thomas estate (TA20 4DD)

Wycliffe

Cornwall

In terms of stunning locations, the ITV detective drama *Wycliffe* was the best television advertisement for the beautiful county of Cornwall since Poldark was filmed by the BBC back in the 70s. Jack Shepherd starred as likeable Cornish sleuth Detective Superintendent Charles Wycliffe alongside his faithful team of Jimmy Yuill and Helen Masters as Detective Inspectors Doug Kersey and Lucy Lane.

Together they solved all manner of baffling cases during the show's five series which ran from a pilot episode in 1993 until 1998. The production base was Truro but locations all over Cornwall from quiet farmhouses and pretty fishing villages to cliffs buffeted by raging seas and upmarket houses were used in the filming of the show.

The dramatic scene in the opening episode when a man walking his dog is gunned down was filmed at Caerhays beach below Caerhays Castle. In another episode a burning wheel was pushed off a stunning peak, actually the National Trust's Pentire Point, a beauty spot much loved by walkers. The wild west theme park featured in the episode The Scapegoat was actually Frontier City near St Columb Major and the whole village of St Ewe was taken over by the film crew for the episode The Last Rites.

Other key scenes were filmed at Porthleven, Redruth, Portreath, Goonhilly Down (the BT communications centre), Carharrach and Kennach Sands. The shot of an exploding fishing boat in the episode The Pea Green Boat was filmed off Godrevy Point near Hayle and a car going off a cliff in the same episode was filmed at Porthowan.

Sat nav reference:

Caerhays Castle (PL26 6LY)

Also in the South West

Echo Beach

The ITV drama starring Martine McCutcheon and Jason Donovan was set in the fictional Cornish town of Polnarren. In actual fact it was filmed in Looe, Polperro and Watergate Bay. Jason Donovan's character's surfboard shop and café was filmed at the Extreme Store, part of the hotel at Watergate Bay (www.watergatebay.co.uk), where scenes were also filmed at its outside bar area. Some of the stars stayed there during filming.

Sat nav reference:

Watergate Bay (TR8 4AA)

Wild West

Filmed at Portloe, on the south Cornwall coast, which doubled as fictional St Gweep, Simon Nye's comedy starred Dawn French as lesbian Mary Trewednack who ran a shop with her partner Angela.

The South East

Agatha Christies Marple
Agatha Christies Poirot
Bleak House
The Darling Buds of May
Downton Abbey
Fawlty Towers
Foyle's War
The Good Life
Holby Blue
Howard's Way
It Ain't Half Hot Mum
Jonathan Creek
Lady Chatterley
Men Behaving Badly
Midsomer Murders
Mrs Brown
The Office
Porridge
The Vicar of Dibley

Agatha Christie's Marple

Chilterns

Along with *Agatha Christie's Poirot*, this hugely successful ITV drama is shot in a wealth of locations across the Chilterns and sometimes beyond. Every film uses a number of locations often spread miles apart, yet as in episodes of *Poirot*, viewers are led to believe every scene has been shot in one place.

For instance, a number of separate houses are used to serve as Rutherford Hall in the 2004 film *4.50 from Paddington*, including Highclere Castle in Hampshire (see *Downton Abbey*), Loseley Park in Guildford and Knebworth House in Stevenage, Hertfordshire www.knebworthhouse.com. Eltham Palace in Court Road, Eltham serves as Noel Coward's House while far further afield in Leicestershire, Rothley Station is Paddington Station in London.

Above: **Holly Willoughby chats to super sleuth Miss Marple (Julia McKenzie) during a break from filming episode *The Pale Horse*.**

So far there have been five series of *Marple*, starting in 2004 with Geraldine McEwan in the title role of Miss Marple, the famous sleuth. Actress Julia McKenzie took over in 2009 for the fourth series and the fifth which was screened in January 2011.

Above: **The beautiful village of Turville, used for Marple and home to *The Vicar of Dibley.***

The list of locations used to film the *Marple* films is far too long to include here in its entirety and many pop up in other shows as they are popular with production companies, usually for their convenience and beauty. For example, the picturesque village of Turville in Buckinghamshire is often used to shoot *Marple* scenes and can also be spotted in episodes of *Midsomer Murders, Lewis* and of course *The Vicar of Dibley* to name but a few.

The Secret of Chimneys which was screened at Christmas 2010 was shot in a number of locations including Hatfield House and once again, Knebworth House which both double for various aspects of Chimneys itself. Hatfield House, a magnificent Jacobean estate in Hatfield, Hertfordshire, was used to shoot the exterior of family house Chimneys. It belongs to the so-called Treasure Houses of England, of which there are only ten and is the home of the 7th Marquess of Salisbury. Elizabeth I spent much of her childhood here and indeed learnt of her accession to the throne while here. See www.hatfield-house.co.uk for more details.

Chimney's interiors were filmed mainly at the superb Knebworth House in nearby Stevenage which has been home to the Lytton family since 1490. The imposing property is in a Tudor Gothic style and well worth a visit. It is open to the public who particularly love its spectacular gardens. It is also popular with production companies with films including parts of *The King's Speech* and *Harry Potter and the Goblet of Fire* being shot there in recent years. See www.knebworthhouse.com for more details.

Other scenes in the film were shot in various locations including Langley Park House, an 18th Century Grade II listed property built as a hunting lodge for the 3rd Duke of Marlborough. The basement doubles up as a series of tunnels which on screen of course are part of Chimneys.

The Pale Horse, was shot at Tudor Manor House Dorney Court (which also pops up in *Midsomer Murders* and was used in the 2009 BBC version of *The Day of the Triffids*), Lincolns Inn and some of Temple. See www.dorneycourt.co.uk

Sat nav references:

Dorney Court (SL4 6QP)

Eltham Palace (SE9 5QE)

Hatfield House (AL9 5NQ)

Highclere Castle (RG20 9RN)

Knebworth House (SG3 6PY)

Lincolns Inn (WC2A 3TL)

Loseley Park (GU3 1HS)

Rothley Station (LE7 7LD)

Agatha Christie's Poirot

Chilterns

Above: **Behind the scenes on *Murder on the Orient Express* members of the crew operate a snow machine to create a snowdrift in Black Park.**

Incredibly, this successful crime drama has been running on ITV since 1989 with actor David Suchet in the title role of fictional detective Hercule Poirot. With 65 films made so far, the list of locations used is vast. Like *Agatha Christie's Marple*, the locations used may be nowhere near each other, yet we the viewers are led to believe the whole story's been shot in the same place.

"Filming is always fragmented, like a jigsaw puzzle," said Location Manager Robin Pim who has worked on a number of recent Poirots. "Everything is shot back to front, upside down, inside out in order to make a story come together. In reality, everything is cherry picked from here and there and nothing is as it seems."

The picturesque village of Hambleden between Marlow in Buckinghamshire and Henley-on-Thames features heavily in *Mrs McGinty's Dead* which was screened in 2008, and indeed has popped up in various Poirots over the years. Tucked in the foothills of the Chilterns, the village is an idyllic cluster of flint cottages, complete with a pub, church and village square. It could have been designed for a drama such as *Poirot*. It is already popular with ramblers who have a number of beautiful walks to choose from.

In the story Hambleden doubles up as the village of Broadhinny where *Poirot* is called in to investigate the murder of a charwoman. As the village is owned by the Hambleden Estate, permission has to be sought from the Estate to film its various properties such as the village stores which can prove prohibitively expensive. Therefore, many of the exteriors and village scenes were shot there, while certain privately owned houses outside the ownership of the Estate, doubled up as the village shop and pub. "We had to be careful what was used in shot," said Robin. "We were lucky that we were able to use some privately owned properties but of course the owners don't necessarily want their homes to become a tourist attraction so they can't be named."

Some of the early *Poirots* were shot far and wide while in the past few years, reduced budgets have meant production crews tend to travel overnight no more than two days per film. Therefore every effort is made to keep filming locations as close to each other as possible, although this is not always the case. For example, locations for the 2007 episode *Mrs McGinty's Dead* include parts of Dover in Kent, West Wycombe Park in Buckinghamshire (always a popular filming choice) and the Bluebell Railway in East Sussex www.bluebell-railway.co.uk which often crops up as it is close to London and comes complete with period stations and rolling stock and was also used for a 1999 ITV version of *The Railway Children*.

Above: **David Suchet as *Poirot* filming *Murder on the Orient Express* on location.**

Freemasons Hall in Great Queen Street, London (see *Spooks*) doubles up as a bank while the Royal Courts of Justice are used for some exteriors and a court scene. A particularly famous Agatha Christie's *Poirot* story is *Murder on the Orient Express* with millions tuning in to ITV1's version when it was screened in December 2010. However, despite appearances the film wasn't shot anywhere near the real train which may surprise fans as it appears beautifully authentic on screen. In fact the carriages used for filming were specially created at Pinewood Studios. The snowdrift scenes where all the passengers (and suspects) find themselves stranded were recreated close to the studios in woods in Black Park. This time, the carriages used were real and 'borrowed' from the Nene Valley Railway, Peterborough. "We made the drifts using sandbags and then powered up the snow machines to create the look we wanted," revealed Chris White the Location Manager on the shoot.

Much of this particular film was also shot on location in Malta. Other locations worth pointing out which feature in other Poirots include Dover Castle for The Clocks, where its tunnels are the perfect backdrop for secret liaisons between officers in the intelligence service; Chenies Manor, Buckinghamshire www.cheniesmanorhouse.co.uk for Hallowe'en Party; Cambridge University for The Case of the Missing Will; Somerset; Brighton and of course abroad.

The interior of Poirot's apartment is a specially constructed set at Pinewood Studios, while the exterior used is actually Florin Court, an art deco block of flats in Charterhouse Square, London.

Sat nav references:

Bluebell Railway (TN22 3QL)

Cambridge University (CB2 1TN)

Charterhouse Square (EC1M 6EA)

Chenies Manor (WD3 6ER)

Dover Castle (CT16 1HU)

Freemasons Hall (WC2B 5AZ)

Royal Courts of Justice (WC2A 2LL)

Bleak House

Hertford

Even audiences who had never thought Charles Dickens could be interesting were captivated by the BBC's adaptation of his classic *Bleak House* which was screened in the autumn of 2005. Penned by the talented Andrew Davies and produced by Nigel Stafford-Clark, their brief from the Head of Drama, Jane Tranter, was for it to be "Bold. Fresh. Imaginative." And it certainly fulfilled the criteria.

What made *Bleak House* so eminently watchable was its large and impressive cast of household names. The American actress Gillian Anderson, of The X-Files fame,was the first to jump aboard as Lady Dedlock, much to the delight of casting director Kate Rhodes James, which left a mere 85 further roles to fill, 40 of them principal characters. After much discussion, sweat and tears, the job was done with such stars as Pauline Collins, Nathaniel Parker, Alun Armstrong, Denis Lawson and Charles Dance to name but a few, all signed up.

With such a massive cast and an ambitious number of hours to shoot, filming locations were more important than ever. Everyone involved realised it would be both time and cost-effective not to move around too much if possible and so it was decided that just one large house with the necessary historical features should be used to film various different locations as opposed to either building a set from scratch or indeed, moving from one venue to another.

Balls Park, a Grade I listed building just outside Hertford proved to be the ideal building for it had everything required to make it a practical first choice. "It even had a room we were able to use as Chancery which is at the heart of *Bleak House* and around which all the various stories revolve," explained Nigel Stafford-Clark.

Right: **Stunning Balls Park in Hertford was a great find by the *Bleak House* location manager and a key location for the series.**

Above: **Caddy Jellyby (Nathalie Press) embraces her mother Mrs Jellyby (Liza Tarbuck) in a scene from *Bleak House*.**

Sat nav references:

Balls Park (SG1 8QE)

Cobham Hall (DA12 3BL)

Luton Hoo (LU1 3TQ)

"The Balls Park mansion has this wood-panelled room which goes up three floors and up to the roof – no one could tell us what it had been used for – but it was just what we needed." So it was here that the likes of the interior of Bleak House itself, Tulkinghorn's offices and even the garrets above Krook's shop which were created in the eaves, came to life so convincingly. The interior of the big court room, Lincoln's Inn Court, was also filmed at Balls Park.

The exterior of Balls Park doubled up as the exterior of Boythorn's house and the 16th Century Ingatestone Hall in Essex served as the exterior of Bleak House. This stunning mansion set in formal gardens is owned by the Petre family, having first been acquired by Sir William Petre in 1539. It has been gradually modernised over the centuries and in 1989 when the 18th Lord inherited the property, he totally renovated it and opened it to the public. Telephone 0844 6626049 for details and opening times. Charles Dickens himself lived in Kent for many years and is known to have strolled through the grounds of the very impressive Cobham Hall, a 12th Century manor house set in 150 acres of Grade II listed parkland. The BBC used the exterior of the very same Cobham Hall as the exterior of Lady Dedlock's home, Chesney Wold. It also served as the exterior of the Inns of Court. The interior of the Hall was also used for some scenes. Go to www.cobhamhall.com to learn more about the Hall's history and for public opening times.

One of the concerns of Location Manager Nick Marshall was finding a suitable location to shoot Dickensian London exteriors but the logistics of them actually being in London would have proved time consuming and expensive. He struck lucky when he came across the perfect location, a discovery he considers one of his "professional highlights." Less than an hour from Balls Park, up the M1 motorway, the old farm yard of Luton Hoo was ingeniously transformed into the cobbled streets of London. This historic Grade I listed building is now a luxury five star hotel but half of the estate is still a working farm which proved perfect for the BBC's needs.

"We had an entirely controlled environment that didn't have problems with modern society taking place around it except for the aeroplane noise around Luton Hoo!" Nick said. "We were able to hire it for six months and do everything we needed to do, exactly how we wanted.

"The art department were able to build around and on top of the majority of the buildings and create our own down town London. We still had to go to a few other places such as Spitalfields in east London which still appears traditionally Georgian/Victorian, but many of our exterior requirements (as well as some interiors) were served by the Luton Hoo estate.

"A lot of the interior of the farm buildings were turned into the ground floor of Krook's and Snagsby's shops for instance, so we didn't have problems with continuity. And of course the existing cobbles among the farm buildings were ready to use as they were. I'd go back to film on the estate in a heartbeat if the right project came about. It has such an interesting history and is one of my favourite places."

The Darling Buds of May

Pluckley

The sleepy village of Pluckley in Kent had never expected the attention that it suddenly received in the summer of 1991. For the instant success of Yorkshire Television's *The Darling Buds of May*, starring the ever-popular David Jason as Pop Larkin, brought hordes of fans into the village, which is said to be one of the most haunted places in Britain.

The quaint, 15th Century Black Horse pub played the Hare and Hounds in the series. "We still get people coming to the village because of *The Darling Buds of May*," said landlord Kevin Savidge. "And they also come here for the ghosts as we're one of the most haunted pubs in the country – and we've been on television quite a lot for that too."

Just across the road is the grocer's shop, which featured in the series, as did Pluckley butcher's shop next door. Nearby St Nicholas' Parish Church became a star attraction in the series when Mariette, played by Catherine Zeta Jones, married Charley (Philip Franks). It was also used when Primrose Larkin (Abigail Rokison) was chasing the Reverend Candy, played by Tyler Butterworth.

Above: (left) **David Jason as Pop Larkin** *(centre)* **The Black Horse pub, which doubled as The Hare and Hounds in the series** *(right)* **Pam Ferris, David Jason and Catherine Zeta Jones.**

Next door to the church is the house that played guide mistress Edith Pilchester's home and opposite the church is the small house, which played Orchard Cottage where the Brigadier, played by Moray Watson, lived. A few doors away is the local school which was used in the series as the village hall.

A few miles away from Pluckley, on the road to Smarden, is Buss Farm, which played the Larkins' Home Farm. But the farm is private and not open to the public and it cannot be seen from the road. However, a classic car rally, in aid of two worthy charities takes place every year at the farm – see www.darlingbudsclassiccarshow.co.uk – so you could catch a glimpse of it and also see Pop Larkin's yellow Rolls Royce and the blue truck which was used for Mariette's wedding.

The Darling Buds of May production team stumbled on the farm after spending two weeks looking for the ideal location. "It was quite difficult to find something that fitted the bill," explained Production Designer Alan Davis. "The problem was that many of the houses had been renovated and dolled up."

The farmhouse still had to be repainted and a modern extension at the back of the house had to be disguised. "We decided to cover the whole thing in Kentish weatherboarding to make it look a bit more rural and in keeping with the local architecture," he said.

Above: **David Jason on location at Buss Farm, the main location for *The Darling Buds of May.***

The next job was to add ivy and dead vine to the house. "We put ivy on to take the edge off the squareness of the place," said Alan. The dead vine went on first and then silk and plastic ivy – all bought by the sackload – was stapled on branch by branch.

The farmyard was Alan's biggest headache as it needed to be filled with 1950s junk. Alan and the show's prop buyer roamed the Kent countryside with a heavy lifting vehicle in convoy hunting for junk and snapped up everything that Pop Larkin would have littering his farmyard.

"We got whatever we could find," said Alan. "We picked up tons of apple boxes, an old tractor, an old conveyer, apple picking ladders, barrels, general scrap metal, lots of oil drums, tyres, an old pitch boiling tank, an old water tank and any farm machinery we saw."

Alan was stumped by just one thing – nettles! Not too many of them, but too few. He explained: "In the book there are references to lots of nettles in amongst the scrap and junk but if there's one thing you can't transplant it is weeds!

"You can't actually dig up some nettles or thistles and put them in a pot and water them and expect them to grow because they never do. There's something about weeds that they just don't like being moved."

Some scenes in later episodes of the show, supposedly in Kent, were actually filmed hundreds of miles away in Yorkshire - to save time and money.

"It's a question of cost," explained David Jason. "The producers found that they could get locations in Leeds that looked like Kent. That way they could save money because they didn't have to ship the crew all the way down to Kent and pay for hotels there. As long as it looks like Kent and can convince us all then that's fine. They are very careful to make sure no one can say: 'That can never be Kent.'"

Sat nav references:

Black Horse pub (TN27 0QS)

St Nicholas' Parish Church (TN27 0QS)

School (TN27 0QS)

Downton Abbey

Newbury

Above: **Magnificent Highclere Castle, home to the Carnarvon family since 1679.**

With its stellar cast including Hugh Bonneville, Dame Maggie Smith and Jim Carter, not to mention its creator and screenwriter, *Gosford Park*'s Lord Julian Fellowes, it was perhaps inevitable ITV1's *Downton Abbey* would become an instant hit when it was first screened in the autumn of 2010.

But it's the glorious setting of magnificent Highclere Castle in Newbury, Hampshire which doubles up as *Downton Abbey* itself which makes the series so memorable, keeping an estimated 10 million viewers glued to seven hour-long episodes. A second, eight-part series is currently planned for autumn 2011 and a one-off Christmas 2011 special will take up where the final episode ends.

With its stunning acres of spectacular parkland, vaulted ceilings, panelled state rooms, 6000-book library and priceless furnishings, family-run Highclere Castle is the ideal screen home of the aristocratic Crawley family around whose lives and those of their servants the Edwardian drama is based.

It's believed Oscar-winning Julian Fellowes wanted Highclere Castle for Downton all along as he is good friends with the Earl and Countess of Carnarvon who reside there, although location director Richard May claimed a country-wide search for the perfect property was conducted. "But Highclere fitted the bill," he said.

Highclere which has belonged to the Carnarvon family since 1679, doubles up as the interior and exterior of *Downton Abbey*, while part of the servants' quarters are a specially constructed set at London's Ealing Studios.

The kitchen yard of the house was partially built on the existing property but amazingly took just a few days to build according to Richard. "And we did a little repainting at the castle; some of the corridors were painted to Edwardian colours," he explained. "We didn't have to touch any of the main rooms except one bedroom belonging to a minor character was painted a darker colour

Above: **From left to right, Jessica Brown Findlay (Lady Sybil Crawley), Michelle Dockery (Lady Mary Crawley) and Laura Carmichael (Lady Edith Crawley), daughters of the house in *Downton Abbey*.**
Right: **A grand affair. The aristocratic Crawley family and their guests on the lawns of Downton Abbey.**

Above: **Samantha Bond plays Lady Rosamund Painswick with Dame Maggie Smith as Violet, Dowager Countess and mother of Robert, Earl of Grantham.** Below: **Master of Downton Abbey Robert Crawley (Hugh Bonneville), the Earl of Grantham.**

because it didn't look right on camera being the light shade it was. Then everything was painted back to how we found it of course. "

Highclere has been home to the 8th Earl and Countess of Carnarvon since 2001 and the home of their ancestors the Herbert family since the 17th Century, although records show the Castle stands on ground dating back to medieval times. The Castle has been described by historians as "the perfect Victorian gem" and is well worth a visit, if only to have a glimpse of some of the splendid rooms featured in the TV series.

Over the centuries the Carnarvons have lavished their wealth on remodelling 150-room Highclere, so making it one of the most spectacular family-owned mansions in the world. Structural changes to the interior of the Castle were completed in 1878 and it became a significant focus of political life during the closing stages of the Victorian age. Later, during the First World War, Highclere was used as a hospital for wounded soldiers and then doubled up as an evacuee base for children in World War II.

Aside from being the ideal filming location, it is used for corporate and private events including weddings. Celebrity couple Peter Andre and Katie Price tied the knot there in the opulent saloon which can be seen from the grand staircase and makes an appearance or two in *Downton Abbey*.

Like most privately owned stately homes, maintaining the 4000-acre estate has become increasingly costly and Lord Carnarvon has the unenviable task of finding the exorbitant sums required for Highclere's upkeep. While the property is far from collapsing, money is desperately needed to restore some of the dilapidated, crumbling balustrades and masonry. Many of the rooms are actually uninhabitable and it's estimated that at least £12m is required to restore the property adequately.

Of course tours of the Castle along with hiring out its wonderful facilities help raise much-needed funds. Tourists may also be interested to learn of a

remarkable Egyptian Exhibition which has transformed the castle's cellars, complete with a replica of the Tomb of Tutankhamun, a mummy, sarcophagus and a number of other treasures. It also includes an engaging 'tour' through the life of the so-called 'cursed' 5th Earl of Carnarvon who funded the search for the real Tomb of Tutankhamun. After many years it was finally discovered in the Valley of Kings by his partner Howard Carter in 1922.

As fans of *Downton Abbey* will recall, north Yorkshire towns including Ripon, Malton and Thirsk are referred to in the series, yet the village of Downton itself where the drama is set, is fictional and indeed could be anywhere. "Finding the village was a huge challenge," Richard May continued. "Finding a village we could have control of to lose things like street markings and lamp posts and so on wasn't easy. We found a village called Bampton in Oxfordshire which proved perfect in the end. The villagers were fantastic, the nicest I've ever worked with actually. They were friendly and helpful and made everything possible."

Even though eagle-eyed viewers have spotted the odd mistake here and there such as a television aerial or conservatory peeping out in some scenes, most would agree Bampton has proved perfect as the Edwardian Downton. Set dressers cleverly covered up street lamps with trees and bushes, yellow lines were disguised and the odd home transformed into a shop or a pub, making the village even more idyllic for screen purposes. Residents of Bampton will recognise their local library which doubles up as the entrance to the cottage hospital as well as St Mary's Church which pops up fairly frequently. Villagers thoroughly enjoyed having camera crews and top name stars in their midst and some were fortunate enough to gain work as supporting artists, while others simply took the opportunity to watch the production team from Carnival Films, at work on their doorstep.

Other locations used in the series include private homes in Bampton for the Rectory and Dower House and St James Park in London where housemaid Anna, played by Joanna Frogatt, can be seen while trying to learn more about Bates' past. Bates himself arrives by train to Downton, a scene filmed at the Kent and East Sussex Railway. www.kesr.org.uk For details of visitor opening times at Highclere Castle and further information, go to www.highclerecastle. co.uk or telephone 01635 253210.

Above (left): **Dame Maggie Smith as the formidable Dowager Countess of Grantham in *Downton Abbey*.**
Above (right): **The staff of Downton Abbey line up to meet their guests.**

Sat nav references:

Bampton (OX18 2NE)

Highclere Castle (RG20 9RN)

Kent and East Sussex Railway (TN30 6HE)

Fawlty Towers

Bourne End

Sadly the real house used on screen as the infamous Fawlty Towers hotel was bulldozed in early 1993. Wooburn Grange at Bourne End in Buckinghamshire, was ravaged by fire in March 1991 just before it was due to be renovated and was hit by a second blaze just four months later. Fawlty Towers hotel was supposed to be in Torquay in Devon but BBC bosses chose the Buckinghamshire site because it was nearer to London. After filming ended Wooburn Grange became a nightclub called Basil's and was later used as an Indian restaurant. By the spring of 1993 it had been demolished completely and had been replaced by eight five-bedroom family homes.

But *Fawlty Towers* fans can however visit other places associated with the series like Mentmore Close in north London where Basil beats his car with the branch of a tree in *Gourmet Night.* Just round the corner in Dovedale Avenue is St John's United Reformed Church which Basil is seen driving past in the same episode and the location for Andre's restaurant was 294 Preston Road in Harrow, which is now a Chinese restaurant called Wings.

The hospital used in *The Germans*, where Sybil has her in-growing toenail removed, is Northwick Park Hospital in Northwick Park. Or you could head off to Torquay where the Gleneagles Hotel, the inspiration for the show, is located. But don't expect Fawlty-style service, for as the hotel says on its website it has "been transformed from a place that inspired the BBC hit TV show *Fawlty Towers* into a modern boutique hotel typical of a place found in the world's most glamorous must visit cities and resorts."
See www.hotel-gleneagles.com

Sat nav references:

Gleneagles Hotel (TQ1 2QS)

Northwick Park Hospital (HA1 3UJ)

Wings (HA3 0QA)

Foyle's War

Hastings

Above: **Michael Kitchen and Honeysuckle Weeks filming in Hastings.**

Foyle's War made its debut on ITV in 2002 and was considered an overnight hit. In fact it was the highest rated drama of that year, pulling in an amazing 10 million viewers and went on to win a BAFTA in 2003.

Written and carefully researched by Anthony Horowitz, who also created the ever popular *Midsomer Murders*, the crime drama is set on the south coast of England during World War II. Series one began in 1940 while the final series six, was set at the end of the war in 1945. Detective Chief Superintendent Christopher Foyle, played by the convincing Michael Kitchen, investigated murders and other serious crime against a backdrop of 1940s England, touching on subjects such as internment and conscription dodging in the process.

The attention to 1940s detail was one of the most impressive factors of *Foyle's War*. The production team went to great lengths to make every

Above: (left) **A prop post box is carried into place** *(centre)* **a bird's eye view of filming** *(right)* **Michael Kitchen and Honeysuckle Weeks filming in Hastings** *(below)* **Michael Kitchen as Christopher Foyle.**

scene as authentic as possible and all evidence of modern day life such as television aerials, satellite dishes, modern streetlamps and burglar alarms had to be removed or disguised from areas used for filming. And of course road markings, street signs and today's cars had to be hidden too.

Christopher Foyle lived in Hastings and it was here that a large chunk of all six series was shot. For instance, Steep Street was the location for Foyle's house and a genuine home – the actual address used was in fact 31 Croft Road, a rather narrow street in the old town. The house was privately owned and let out to ITV for filming purposes.

The High Street, Post Office Passage and Church Street also regularly cropped up in every series and like Croft Road, are narrow and restrictive and were usually closed off to the public while filming, not that residents raised objections. St Clements Church which can be found just off the High Street made regular appearances in *Foyle's War* as Sam (Honeysuckle Weeks) had to drive past it every time she visited Foyle at home. It was also used for a scene on a National Day of Prayer in one episode.

The pilot of *Foyle's War*, which was made in the summer of 2001, was shot in old town Hastings which proved to be an excellent choice of location. The beautiful beach with its close proximity to France and historic links to the war led Anthony Horowitz to make his lead character a Hastings resident and so a firm bond between Foyle and the town was forged.

Simon Allen, Film Liaison Officer for Hastings Borough Council, said the town grew to love *Foyle's War* over the years and like audiences worldwide, were saddened when the final episodes were filmed in 2007. However, the good news is that Anthony Horowitz has stated that he hasn't ruled out writing further episodes at some point so it may not be the end for *Foyle's War* after all.

Historic landmarks, the fishermen's net huts appeared in some episodes as did Hastings Pier which first opened in 1872. The Royal Victoria Hotel, St Leonards was the scene of a murder following a bombing raid. While filming took place, the A259 which runs outside the hotel, was temporarily closed – no small feat as it happens to be one of the busiest roads in the UK.

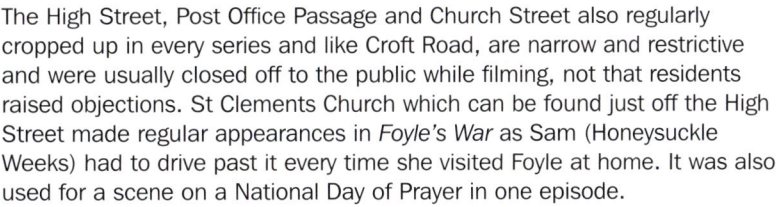

Above: **Actors playing soldiers on Hastings beach.**

Other locations used to shoot *Foyle's War* included Squerryes Court in Westerham, Kent, a stunning 17th Century manor house surrounded by 20 acres of historic gardens. Telephone 01959 562345 or see www.squerryes. co.uk for information on opening times.

The market town of Midhurst, West Sussex was chosen to film an episode in series five and locals recall seeing the actors huddled under umbrellas in the March of 2006 as the rain poured down. Several locations in the town were employed, including Midhurst Bookshop in Knockhundred Row which became a hairdressers in the drama. The house adjoining the bookshop, Burgage House, was used as the Southern Bank.

Sat nav references:

Burgage House (GU29 9DQ)

Midhurst Bookshop (GU29 9DQ)

The Royal Victoria Hotel (TN38 0BD)

St Clements Church (TN34 3EY)

Squerryes Court (TN16 1SJ)

The Good Life

Northwood

The classic 70s comedy *The Good Life* sees Tom and Barbara Good turn their middle class home in Surbiton into a self-sufficient empire of vegetables and animals. At the time, it caused thousands to copy their idea and countless lawns all over the country were dug up and replaced by rows of carrots and turnips. Tom and Barbara's lifestyle, however, was far from ideal for their upmarket next-door neighbours Margo and Gerry Leadbetter, played by Penelope Keith and Paul Eddington, who awoke each morning to the sound of pigs and hens. In the series Kewferry Road in Northwood, Middlesex doubled for the fictional road, The Avenue, Surbiton, Surrey, because it was easier for the crew and actors to travel from the BBC Television Centre to Northwood with their cameras and props than Surbiton. Finding two suitable houses side by side for the series, one slightly run-down and one immaculate could have been a problem but location managers struck lucky in Kewferry Road.

"They were very lucky," recalled Richard Briers. "Tom and Barbara's house was 1930s and a bit peeling and a little bit shabby and Gerry and Margo's was one of those Hendon type houses, very smart with bay windows and with a much smarter garden so we didn't have to do anything to it which was very lucky." Of course, the then owners of the Goods' house, Number 55, had agreed to have both their fully-lawned front and back gardens dug up and covered with vegetables not to mention having animals running round - and one of their rooms doubling up as a make-up and costume store. After each series a BBC crew dug up the vegetables and re-laid the turf - and after the final series the production team even added a patio for them.

Sat nav reference:

Kewferry Road, Northwood (HA6 2PQ)

Holby Blue

Surrey

Following the success of hospital dramas *Casualty* and *Holby City*, Kudos decided to produce spin-off cop drama *Holby Blue* in 2007 with a host of well-known names including Zoe Lucker and James Thornton. However, unlike the former series which continue to be successful, the show didn't take off and was axed the following year after just two seasons.

Holby Blue was set in Holby Police Station which was actually filmed on a purpose-built set at a former Ministry of Defence complex near Chertsey.The exterior of the station was shot at Brunel University in west London. Some of the cast spent time at nearby Woking Police Station shadowing uniformed officers. The towns of Chertsey, Woking and Egham were all used for exterior scenes such as car chases and gun battles.

Sat nav references:

Brunel University (UB8 3PH)

Woking Police Station (GU22 7AE)

Howard's Way

Bursledon

Above: ***Howard's Way*** **was usually filmed in Hampshire, but this picture of stars Tony Anholt, Jan Harvey, Ivor Danvers, Kate O'Mara and Stephen Yardley was taken on location in Malta.**

Sat nav references:

Elephant Boatyard (SO31 8DN)

The Jolly Sailor (SO31 8DN)

St Leonard's Church (SO31 8DU)

The BBC's 80s sex and sailing soap *Howard's Way* brought tourists flocking to south Hampshire where the series was filmed. It was set around the fictional village of Tarrant, played in real life by pretty Bursledon near Southampton. The series focused on the Mermaid Boatyard owned by Tom Howard and Jack Rolfe and that was played by the Elephant Boatyard in Land's End Road. You can still enjoy a quiet drink or a meal at the main pub used in *Howard's Way*, The Jolly Sailor just along the road. Halfway down Kew Road is Bondfield House, a private house which played the Howard family home in the series and just off Kew Lane is Hungerford where Hunt's Folly played the home of Jan's mother Kate Harvey. The other major location was St Leonard's Church in Church Lane, Hamble, which was used for the filming of Lynne Howard and Claude Dupont's wedding.

The BBC was very resourceful in its use of locations to save money, for example the Victoria Rampart Jetty at nearby Warsash doubled as New York harbour when Lynne Howard crossed the Atlantic single-handedly, the High Street at Hamble played Italy in one episode and Waddesdon Manor, a National Trust property near Aylesbury, Buckinghamshire played Charles Frere's French Chateau Auban. Exterior shots of Victoria Rampart offices were also used as Ken Master's chandlery and Jan Howard's boutique and scenes at Ken's powerboat centre were filmed at a real-life showroom on the A27 at Swanwick. The business park built by tycoon Charles Frere in the series was actually Arlington Securities' Solent Business Park, just off junction nine of the M27 and the marina that Frere builds was actually Hythe Marina, at Hythe, near Southampton.

It Ain't Half Hot Mum

Farnham

You could be mistaken for thinking that the BBC comedy *It Ain't Half Hot Mum*, which was set in wartime Burma, was actually filmed in a hot sticky climate. But that was just clever make-up. For the series, featuring the exploits of an army concert party, was actually filmed at BBC studios with the furthest location used being woods at Farnham in Surrey. And as with *Dad's Army*, the MoD allowed the BBC to film on its land, this time a wood. Clever set-dressing turned Farnham into Burma. Writer Jimmy Perry recalled: "We used to put rubber palms and rubber jungle creepers in the ground." The late Ken MacDonald, best-known as barman Mike Fisher in *Only Fools and Horses* was thrilled when he was given the part of banjo-playing Gunner Clark, particularly at the thought of filming in some exotic foreign location. "But we ended up in these woods in Farnham," he recalled in 1993. "But it was a great show to get into and tremendous fun." And although Michael Knowles, who plays dashing Captain Ashwood, loved working on the show, he doesn't miss the daily routine he faced on the set of *It Ain't Half Hot Mum* - being covered in fake sweat. "It was agony," he said. "We had a lot of lighting to make it look hot and they used to spray this glycerine and water stuff on us and the sand would blow up and stick on you."

Jonathan Creek

Shipley

Jonathan Creek isn't your average television detective and it's therefore quite apt that he doesn't have a typical home. In fact Jonathan's home couldn't really have been more unusual. After all, how many other television characters live in a windmill? In David Renwick's cleverly crafted mystery series, the eponymous hero, played by Alan Davies and his investigative crime writer colleagues solves seemingly impossible crimes.

Originally the production team making *Jonathan Creek* hoped to find a windmill near to their base at Teddington Studios but that didn't work out as Production Designer John Asbridge explained: "Our location manager had been driving round the countryside but it soon became apparent that we were going to go away from London for the mill because we just couldn't find what we needed that close to London because by their very nature these places tend to be out in the countryside.

"Even after we starting looking a bit further afield it took some time to find the right mill. Some were cheek-by-jowl with a modern bungalow or house, others had been desperately converted and were just miserable with awful double-glazing. The other problem was if people were living in the mill we knew we'd have to have them out and we'd then have to totally redecorate and furnish what essentially was their home.

"We didn't consider building the interior of Creek's mill as a set because it would be such an expensive set to build, as it would be on three levels and the

Opposite page: **Jonathan Creek star Alan Davies on location at Shipley Windmill.** *Below:* **Stunning Shipley Windmill, the location for Jonathan Creek.**

very nature of the shape of the mill and the way the staircases work in a mill would make it difficult. In addition if we wanted to show off and enjoy any of the redundant workings of the mill like the wheels and the cogs then that would have been very expensive to recreate."

Eventually the location manager discovered Shipley Mill in west Sussex, a former home of the writer Hilaire Belloc, which is now owned by a Trust and therefore not lived in. Tucked away down a quiet lane and overlooking a meadow, it was just what the production team needed.

Despite its looks, it's actually the youngest – and the largest – windmill in Sussex having been built in 1879 for a Mr Frend Marten by Horsham millwrights Grist and Steele and cost £2,500. In 1906 the mill, nearby Kings Land house and the surrounding land were bought by Hilaire Belloc. With the advent of freely available electricity and motor vehicles, windmills across Britain began to be used less often as they became uneconomic to run.

Shipley Mill however combated this for a while by having a steam engine fitted that enabled it to be used on days when there was no wind and the mill continued to be used until the end of its active life in 1926.

Finally big roller mills put windmills like Shipley out of business. Between the wars Hilaire Belloc tried to keep the windmill in good order but the shortage of materials during the Second World War meant that by the time of Belloc's death in 1953 it needed considerable work to halt its decline.

An appeal was launched to restore the mill as a memorial to Hilaire Belloc and a local committee was formed which gained the support of the West Sussex County Council and it was reopened in 1958. In 1986 major repairs were again needed and a charitable Trust was formed consisting of various council representatives, the Friends of Shipley Windmill, the Society for the Protection of Ancient Buildings, the Book Trust and Charles Eustace, Belloc's great grandson who has given the Trust a 20-year lease at a peppercorn rent.

In 1990, thanks to grants and donations, the mill was re-opened, with just a single pair of sails, but a year later further donations meant a second pair could be added, restoring the mill to its former glory. Shipley Windmill is no longer open to the public although it may be viewed externally from the adjacent public footpath. See www.shipleywindmill.org.uk for details.

Lady Chatterley

The Isle of Wight

The Isle of Wight doubled for the South of France for the controversial 1993 BBC production of *Lady Chatterley* which starred Joely Richardson in the title role and Sean Bean as her gardener Mellors. The Old Park Hotel at St Lawrence (01983 852583) was the location for the beach and woodland walk scenes and the clifftop theme park, Blackgang Chine and Lisle Combe, the house at the Rare Breeds and Waterfowl Park at St Lawrence, played Lady Chatterley's father's south of France home, Mandalay.

Havenstreet Station, part of the Isle of Wight Steam Railway, which runs from Wootton to Smallbrook Junction featured in the final episode when Lady Chatterley returns home from France.

The final scene where Mellors and Connie embrace at the stern of a ship as they set off for Canada, was filmed on the Southampton to Isle of Wight Red Funnel ferry Cowes Castle which is now no longer in service with the company. The ship doubled as a cross-channel cruise liner sailing from Southampton water. It was picked because it had a traditional wooden handrail and by cleverly filming from different angles Director Ken Russell was able to make the ferry look like a liner.

Sat nav references:

Blackgang Chine (PO38 2HN)

Havenstreet Station (PO33 4DS)

Lisle Combe (PO38 1UW)

Old Park Hotel (PO38 1XS)

Men Behaving Badly

Worthing

The town of Worthing in west Sussex featured heavily in the second episode of the final trilogy of the hilarious BBC comedy *Men Behaving Badly*, broadcast over three nights during Christmas 1998. The story saw Gary, played by Martin Clunes, having to attend a security equipment conference in the town and his girlfriend Dorothy (Caroline Quentin), pal Tony (Neil Morrissey) and his girlfriend Deborah (Leslie Ash) decide to come along too.

They stay at the aptly named Groyne View Hotel in Worthing, which isn't the most romantic venue for a seaside break, especially when all four of them are sharing one room with peeling wallpaper. And while Tony, Dorothy and Deborah entertain themselves during the day with crazy golf, Gary becomes preoccupied with an attractive female delegate at the conference. Tony and Deborah step in to save Gary and Dorothy's relationship and the crazy golf course comes off worst.

In real life the building used as the Groyne View Hotel isn't a hotel at all and is actually flats at 3-10 Marine Parade. It was the perfect setting as the building used to be a three-star hotel.

The pier was used, as was the beach just to the east of the pier where Tony and Gary get drunk in a mock-up car. Flash Point, at the end of the promenade, was also used for the crazy golf course where Gary and Tony have a fight.

Midsomer Murders

Chilterns

Above: **DS Benjamin Jones (Jason Hughes), DCI Tom Barnaby (John Nettles) and DCI John Barnaby (Neil Dudgeon) in a rare appearance together.**

The fictional village of Midsomer may well be one of the most idyllic in England but appearances can be deceptive: it also happens to boast the highest murder rate per manicured acre anywhere with one unfortunate resident after another, bumped off at an alarming rate.

But as luck would have it, in the long-running crime drama series *Midsomer Murders*, there's always been a dependable detective on hand to find the culprit, in the shape of Detective Chief Inspector Tom Barnaby, played by John Nettles since the show began in 1997.

In March 2011 Tom left for pastures new and his equally reliable and tenacious cousin John Barnaby (actor Neil Dudgeon) took over as DCI and is now solving murders which continue to occur at an alarming rate.

The village of Turville, Buckinghamshire, crops up in Murder on *St. Malley's Day*, *Who Killed Cock Robin* and *The Straw Woman*. It's doubly interesting as the popular comedy *The Vicar of Dibley* was also shot there. Look out for the beautiful St Mary the Virgin church in the centre of the village.

Also in Buckinghamshire, this time in Beaconsfield, Barnaby and his team are to be found investigating a gruesome murder in Bekonscot Model Village which doubles up as Little Worthy Model Village in the aptly titled episode *Small Mercies*. Viewers will recall how the victim was discovered tied down among the tiny properties, Gulliver-style.

Equally at home on the cover of a chocolate box and in the same county is Long Crendon which can be seen in *Garden of Death*, *Tainted Fruit, Death & Dreams, Things that go bump... Dead Letters, A Tale of Two Hamlets* and *Second Sight*. Tucked away is the High Street with an array of quaint pubs, shops and cottages. The village courthouse at the end of the High Street features in at least one *Midsomer* episode.

Above (top): **John Nettles and Jason Hughes filming** *The Great and The Good* (above) **Barnaby investigates a gruesome scene at Little Worthy Village, played by Bekonscot Model Village in** *Small Mercies* (opposite) **DS Benjamin Jones (Jason Hughes) DCI John Barnaby (Neil Dudgeon) and Dr George Bullard (Barry Jackson).**

Waddesdon Manor which is situated between Aylesbury and Bicester in Buckinghamshire, a French-style chateau built by the banker, Baron Ferdinand de Rothschild can be spotted in *Death of a Stranger*. With its splendid gardens, it is perfect for weddings, corporate events or just to visit. Go to www.waddesdon.org.uk for further information.

Several picturesque pubs feature in *Midsomer Murders*, including The Cock & Rabbit in Lee in Buckinghamshire where Barnaby enjoys more than a pint or two; The Crown in Cuddington which crops up in *Death in Disguise, Death of a Stranger, Death and Dreams* and *Bad Tidings*; The Plough in Great Haseley, Oxfordshire; the renowned George and Dragon in Quainton, Buckinghamshire and in the same county, The Bell in Chearsley, which doubles up as The Woodman in one episode.

Not surprisingly with so many murders, there have been a fair few funerals in the deathly drama and an array of different churches used to send off the departed as well as for weddings and village gatherings.

Churches featured so far include Beaconsfield Church, Buckinghamshire which has been used as two different churches in different episodes; the interiors of Bray Church in Berkshire for a bell ringing scene; the 14th Century Brightwell Baldwin Church in Oxfordshire spotted in a few different episodes; the church at Brill, Buckinghamshire which features in *Four Funerals and a Wedding* and St Mary's Church in Haddenham, Buckinghamshire which again can be seen in *Judgement Day, A Talent for Life, Birds of Prey, Orchid Fatalis* and *Vixen's Run*. Bledlow Church in the same county, doubled up as Badgers Drift Church in *The Killings at Badgers Drift*.

The secluded and pretty village of Bledlow also pops up in other *Midsomer* episodes, *Dead Man's Eleven, Blue Herrings, Dark Autumn* and *The Maid in Splendour* and interestingly, also in at least one episode of *Agatha Christie's Miss Marple*.

The church of St Peter & St Paul in Dinton, Buckinghamshire which dates back to the 15th Century is used for a wedding scene in *Who Killed Cock Robin*, while in nearby Westlington Green, a body is found in a well in *Dead Letters*. On a happy note, at least for Tom Barnaby who rarely has much good news in his line of work, St Mary's Parish Church in Denham, Buckinghamshire, is used to film his screen daughter Cully's (Laura Howard) wedding to Simon Dixon, played by Sam Hazeldine in the episode entitled somewhat chillingly, *Blood Wedding*.

And don't forget, it's worth visiting all these beautiful villages for their wealth of history, interesting shops and quaint houses – all reasons which brought *Midsomer Murders* to their doorsteps.

Other locations worth mentioning include lovely Loseley Park near Guildford, Surrey www.loseleypark.co.uk where a large chunk of episode *They Seek Him Here* was shot in early 2008. (This is not the first time Loseley has appeared in the series and indeed, it is a popular filming venue for many television dramas and films.) The historic estate doubles up as Magna Manor, a shooting location for a film of *The Scarlet Pimpernel*. The director is found guillotined and Barnaby is called in to track down the murderer.

Estate owner Michael More-Molyneux said the *Midsomer* team used Loseley to the full, filming in its driveways and passages and stable yard which doubled up as a French courtyard complete with guillotine and chickens in cages.

"It was all very authentic looking because the production brought in all their own props and furniture including street lamps," said Mr More-Molyneux. "They were here for some days and really employed Loseley well using every bit of the estate. It was an enjoyable experience all round; they really were a super crew."

Loseley, which celebrated its 500th anniversary in 2008, is open to visitors to enjoy its surroundings and for celebratory and corporate events. Telephone the Estate Office on 01483 304440 for details of opening times.

John Nettles' final *Midsomer* episode, *Fit for Murder* is set in a beautiful health spa. Sadly, there's no point in trying to book a getaway as the 'spa' is in fact a privately owned former manor house, now converted into a classically-designed office block just a stone's throw from Pinewood Studios in Buckinghamshire. The building is currently empty and awaiting redevelopment.

Neil Dudgeon's first episode as DCI John Barnaby, *Death in the Slow Lane*, which kicked off series 14, employed a girls' private school near Reading as an exclusive school in the plot. The school (the head prefers it not to be named) was taken over by the production during the school holidays and interestingly was also used in a previous *Midsomer* episode, *Murder on St. Malley's Day*.

Neil's second *Midsomer* film features a location fans can happily visit, Mapledurham House, Mapledurham in Oxfordshire. The estate doubles up as the home of an eccentric couple (played by Phyllida Law and Edward Fox) in *Dark Secrets* and boasts a working watermill which is well worth a look. Go to www.mapledurham.co.uk for details of opening times.

Fans of *Midsomer Murders* reading this may well wonder why a location known to them hasn't been mentioned here. As stated earlier, there have been far too many over the years to include but here are a few more for the record: Dorney Court, Berkshire is used in several episodes including *Dark Secrets*; Buckinghamshire Railway Station (seen in *Things that Go Bump in the Night* and *Down among the Dead*); the Watercress Line, a beautiful steam railway which runs through the heart of Hampshire and is used in *Echoes of the Dead*; Holloway College, Egham, Surrey; the Henley Regatta at Oxfordshire; the Tiptree Jam Factory in Essex; Chalgrove Manor, Oxfordshire and Chenies Manor, Chenies, Buckinghamshire www.cheniesmanorhouse.co.uk

Sat nav references:

The Bell (HP18 0DJ)

Bledlow Church (HP27 9PD)

Brightwell Baldwin Church (OX49 5NS)

Buckinghamshire Railway Station (HP22 4BY)

Chalgrove Manor (OX44 7SL0)

Chenies Manor (WD3 6ER)

The Church at Brill (HP18 9RT)

The Cock & Rabbit (HP16 9LZ)

The Crown (HP18 0BB)

Dorney Court (SL4 6QP)

George and Dragon (HP22 4AR)

Loseley Park (GU3 1HS)

Mapledurham House (RG4 7TR)

The Plough (OX44 7JP)

St Mary's Church (OX9 3AJ)

St Mary's Parish Church (WD3 1JB)

St Peter & St Paul Church (HP17 8UG)

Tiptree Jam Factory in Essex (CO5 0RF)

Waddesdon Manor (HP18 0JH)

Mrs Brown

The Isle of Wight

Much of the BBC film *Mrs Brown*, which tells the poignant and unusual love story between Queen Victoria, played by Dame Judi Dench, and her loyal Highland ghillie John Brown, played by Billy Connolly, took place at Queen Victoria and Prince Albert's real-life retreat, Osborne House on the Isle of Wight.

Victoria married Albert in 1840, three years after she had come to the throne and they bought the site in 1845 and replaced the existing house with Thomas Cubitt's design for a new home, the building that we see now. It was completed in 1851 and is now in the care of English Heritage. See www.english-heritage.org.uk for details.

The Royal couple found tranquillity at Osborne House with its fine views across the Solent and elegant Italian style away from the formality of court life at Buckingham Palace and Windsor Castle. Victoria said of it: "It is impossible to imagine a prettier spot."

Above: **Osborne House, one of the main settings in *Mrs Brown*.**

Queen Victoria died on 22nd January 1901 on a couch bed in the Queen's Bedroom. The private royal suite was closed to all except members of the royal family until Queen Elizabeth II gave permission for full public access in 1954.

Of course much of *Mrs Brown* was filmed in Scotland. Privately owned 14th Century Duns Castle, on the Scottish borders near the market town of Duns, had a prominent role and if you fancy living like royalty, the castle offers accommodation and is available for weddings. See www.dunscastle.co.uk for more details.

Queen Victoria's waterfall picnic was filmed at a waterfall on the River Pattack near Loch Laggan. Other scenes were shot at Wilton House, Wilton, Wiltshire, which has also been used for the films *Sense and Sensibility*, *The Madness of King George* and *Pride and Prejudice*. See www.wiltonhouse.co.uk for details.

Osterley Park House, Isleworth, Middlesex, which also appeared in *Cranford*, was also used as was Luton Hoo, in Bedfordshire, a veteran of more than 20 films and TV shows including the Bond film *The World Is Not Enough*, *Four Weddings and a Funeral* and *Bleak House*.

Sat nav references:

Duns Castle (TD11 3NW)

Luton Hoo (LU1 3TQ)

Osborne House (PO32 6JX)

Osterley Park House (TW7 4RB)

Wilton House (SP2 0BJ)

The Office

Slough

The Office certainly put Slough on the map with millions of television viewers – but perhaps not in a way that the Berkshire town's local council might have liked, as it doesn't exactly suggest it is a happening place. Of course Ricky Gervais and Stephen Merchant's brilliant workplace spoof fly-on-the-wall comedy was mainly filmed at Teddington Studios but the show's iconic opening title sequence was shot in Slough.

Right: **Crossbow House in Slough, used as the exterior for *The Office*.**

The Brunel bus station and car park appeared (now demolished) as does the nearby Brunel Roundabout. The building on the Slough Trading Estate used for the exterior for the Wernham Hogg office in the opening titles was Crossbow House, Liverpool Road, Slough, although there is talk of the area being redeveloped in the future which could see Crossbow House disappearing which would be a shame as it is one of the most recognisable buildings on television.

Sat nav reference:

Crossbow House (SL1 4QZ)

Porridge

St Albans

Above: **The exterior for Slade Prison in St Albans - now a register office.**

Ball and chain jokes often feature at weddings at St Albans Register Office in Victoria Street, but that's perhaps predictable as it is housed in the former gatehouse to St Albans Prison. But the register office has an even greater claim to fame – it was the setting for the classic television comedy *Porridge* where Norman Stanley Fletcher does his lengthy stretch. The real Victorian St Albans Prison, which had room for 85 men and 14 women, saw four executions, the last one being in 1914, but it hadn't been used as a real prison for decades when the BBC borrowed it as the front of HM Prison Slade. Designers put up the Slade signs, barred nearby windows and built a set of double doors at the end of the gatehouse entrance tunnel. The gatehouse was used after the Home Office refused to allow the BBC to film at an actual prison. Exterior scenes set within the walls of Slade Prison were filmed at various psychiatric hospitals around London.

It became St Albans Register Office in 2004 after being home to St Albans Highways Department for many years and offices have now been built behind the gatehouse. "We trade on the *Porridge* connection and it is known locally as the old Porridge building," said Deputy Superintendent Registrar Claire Cook. "We still have the old prison doors which are attractive for photographs when they are closed. People – usually grooms – constantly make jokes about it being appropriate to get married at an old prison!"

The Home Office has relaxed its ban on filming in prisons since *Porridge* began in 1974 and now allows television companies to film in prisons for a fee, although much of the ITV drama hit *Bad Girls* was filmed at former Oxford Prison, which has now been converted into a hotel. See www.oxfordprison.co.uk for details.

Sat nav reference:

St Albans Register Office (AL1 3TF)

The Vicar of Dibley

Turville

Above: **The beautiful village of Turville which plays Dibley.**
Right: **St Mary The Virgin Church in Turville, which plays St Barnabus in** *The Vicar of Dibley.*

The BBC comedy series *The Vicar of Dibley* became a huge hit for the BBC and creator Richard Curtis. It stars Dawn French as Dibley vicar Reverend Geraldine Granger, whose pastoral work isn't always easy in a village full of quirky characters like Hugo (James Fleet), Alice (Emma Chambers), Owen (Roger Lloyd Pack) and Jim (Trevor Peacock).

Exterior scenes for the series were filmed in the Buckinghamshire village of Turville with the local church St Mary The Virgin, which dates back to the 12th Century, doubling as fictional St Barnabus Church. The exterior for the screen vicarage was actually two cottages in the village which were made to look like one house, but interior shots were filmed weeks later at the BBC studios in London, with a fake backdrop in place at the front door for continuity.

Turville is no stranger to film crews as a nearby windmill which overlooks the village, was used for the classic 1968 film *Chitty Chitty Bang Bang,* which stars Dick Van Dyke and Sally Ann Howes, and for the 1996 live action version of 101 Dalmatians.

Sat nav reference:
St Mary The Virgin Church (HP22 5SH)

Also in the South West

The Brittas Empire

The BBC comedy about the exploits of Whitbury Leisure Centre manager Gordon Brittas, played by Chris Barrie, was filmed at Ringwood Recreation Centre at Ringwood in Hampshire. The centre remained open to the public even when the series was being filmed between 1991 and 1997. "We'd book the sports hall for a day just like anyone else would," recalled producer Mike Stephens. "And the same with the pool and the rest of it."

The location was picked for two reasons, as Mike explained: "Basically I wanted somewhere that looked different and it has certainly got a different style to it and also Chris was appearing in a play at Winchester while we were filming so we needed to find somewhere that he could get to easily each day."

Sat nav reference:

Ringwood Recreation Centre (BH24 1PX)

Above: **Alex Ferns starred as a Royal Navy captain in *Making Waves*.**

Making Waves

ITV had high hopes for its Royal Navy drama *Making Waves* - and so they should have. After all the Ministry of Defence had loaned producers a huge prop - Type 23 frigate HMS Grafton to play fictional HMS Suffolk and the show was blessed with a solid cast including former *EastEnders* star Alex Ferns as Suffolk's CO. But the series bombed and unusually was taken off air before all of its six episodes had been screened. The cast and crew had spent many months filming the multi-million pound show in Portsmouth at the Dockyard and at other locations all over the city including the popular Gunwharf Quays shopping and restaurant waterfront development. For details see www.gunwharf-quays.com

Ruth Rendell Inspector Wexford Mysteries

Most major towns in Hampshire were used at some point for the filming of the *Ruth Rendell Inspector Wexford Mysteries* which began in 1988 and ran until 2000. The country detective, played by veteran actor George Baker, is based at Kingsmarkham played by the town of Romsey near Southampton. The side entrance of the town's Magistrates Court doubled as the entrance to the police station with the production team adding just a sign and putting police cars in the car park to make it look like the real thing.

Many streets in the centre of Romsey featured in the stories and most restaurants and cafes were seen at some point along with the Job Centre, Romsey Abbey, the Corn Market and Palmerston Square. Two pubs, the Queen Vic and the King William IVth played Wexford's locals and the house that played his home was also in the town. Outside Romsey, St John's Church at Farleigh Chamberlayne near Braishfield was used for a funeral scene, an Indian restaurant called Kuti's in London Road, Southampton, was used for one episode, Sherfield Parish Hall doubled as a police control centre and Southampton University was used as Brighton University.

Interior scenes for the story Speaker of Mandarin, which were supposed to be at a hotel in China, were actually shot at the Botley Park Hotel in Botley. The Kings Theatre in Southsea played a cinema and The Fuzz and Furkin pub, a former real police station, in Albert Road, Southsea, played a police station.

Sat nav references:

Botley Park Hotel (SO32 2UA)

The Kings Theatre (PO5 2SH)

King William IVth (SO51 8DF)

Kuti's (SO14 3DP)

Romsey Abbey (SO51 8EP)

Sherfield Parish Hall (RG27 0AA)

Southampton University (SO17 1BJ)

London

Ashes to Ashes
The Bill
Eastenders
Holby City
Goodnight Sweetheart
London's Burning
Silk
Spooks

Ashes to Ashes

London

For the millions who adored *Life on Mars*, the follow up *Ashes to Ashes* was eagerly awaited and sparked an on-going debate as to whether the latter is as good as the former. Whatever one's opinion, this series paid just as much attention to period detail in its locations, being set in 1980s London, as opposed to 1970s Manchester.

Life on Mars featured Sam Tyler, a modern detective who finds himself back in 1973 after a car crash, and *Ashes to Ashes* worked on the same premise except this time, DI Alex Drake, a bright, feisty psychological profiler played by Keeley Hawes, is propelled from 2008 back to 1981. Here she teamed up with the ever-macho Detective Chief Inspector Gene Hunt (Philip Glenister) and theirs proved an often tempestuous pairing.

Above: **Philip Glenister as DCI Gene Hunt, Keeley Hawes as DI Alex Drake and the famous Audi Quattro in a scene from *Ashes to Ashes*.**

Three main locations which featured regularly throughout the series – CID, Alex's flat and Luigis restaurant - were all sets built at Kudos's production space in Bermondsey, south east London.

"It's in the same space as *Spooks* actually," revealed Mark Grimwade, who was Location Manager for some of *Ashes to Ashes* series one. "They would move out, we would move in and when we had moved out, *Hustle* would move in so they have (production company Kudos) got a permanent build space where they take one set down and put up another."

The exterior of the police station in *Ashes to Ashes* was actually shot at an empty building owned by the Stock Exchange on Christopher Street, EC2, London, by Finsbury Square. And conveniently, on the same street is a restaurant called Alexander's which played as Luigis.

"With any exteriors you have to find buildings that are pre-1980s which can be anything from 100 years old up to 1981 so it can be quite difficult to find. A lot of *Ashes to Ashes* was based around the river and the docks and to find those sorts of places which haven't been developed is pretty tricky," said Mark.

"It was also meant to be based all around the Docklands area in east London and of course a lot of that has been developed. You just find certain streets which have parts that are still old fashioned and you have to be clever with the camera as to what you point at and what you don't."

Fans of the show will recall scenes on the River Thames which were shot near London's Royal Docks when Hunt and the boys race to Alex's rescue on a speed boat at the end of the first episode. Old, disused mills doubled up as wharf-side buildings with Tower Bridge as the backdrop.

Other locations used include a club next door to Caesar's (London's oldest nightclub) in Streatham Hill. It was here that a gay club scene was shot. In another episode, the real Steve Strange, a club scene fixture in the 80s, was invited to the Blitz Club. This was in fact a snooker hall dressed to recreate the famous club and real Blitz Club fans appear as very enthusiastic extras with 80s perms, shoulder pads or 'new romantic' costumes.

Mark said part of the struggle with shooting period drama in the streets is clearing it of modern day cars which have to be replaced with period cars. Residents in selected areas such as Lewisham, large sections of which haven't been gentrified, received letters asking them to move their vehicles.
"Most of the time they were very co-operative and didn't mind helping us," he said "When a parked car couldn't be moved for any reason, we had to park a period car in front of it.

Sat nav references:

Alexander's (EC2A 2BS)

Caesar's (SW2 4RU)

"We shot a lot in Southwark and they're brilliant. Some councils are less keen on the idea of filming but luckily, Southwark are happy about it and without their help, making *Ashes to Ashes* just wouldn't have been possible."

The Bill

Merton

Above: **The exterior of Sun Hill police station in *The Bill*.**

This popular cop drama was axed in August 2010 after 26 years, during which time Sun Hill became television's best known police station. When *The Bill* began filming in 1984, the production base was a single-story office and warehouse complex in Artichoke Hill, Wapping in east London. In 1986 a redbrick, former record company distribution warehouse in Barlby Road, north Kensington became Sun Hill number two. The Victorian building, with an arched doorway, was well suited to its role and became a popular home for the series among both actors and production team. When Thames TV's lease on the building ran out in 1989 the owners announced that they were going to turn the site into a shopping centre and *The Bill* had to look for a new home.

Production company Thames TV decided upon a former wine warehouse in Deer Park Road, Merton which remained home to the long-running show until its demise. The new studio was bigger than the two previous ones which enabled the series to grow as the programme developed considerably over the years. Extra sets were added such as a courtroom and the fictional St Hugh's Hospital where many a victim of crime found themselves.

EastEnders

Borehamwood

Above: **It all looks so real - but Albert Square is a specially built set at a studio at Borehamwood, Hertfordshire.**

EastEnders is a problem for location fans because there is very little for them to actually see as the show is shot almost entirely on a specially built set at BBC Elstree in Borehamwood, Hertfordshire.

The construction of the set took place between May and November 1984. The show's original design team wanted Albert Square to look old and established and as authentic as possible.

At the same time, they were concerned that the 'fake' buildings would not to be able to withstand the ravages of the British climate and didn't hold out much hope of them lasting more than three years. Little did they know, more than two decades later, the original Albert Square would still be standing.

Said the late designer Keith Harris: "After the hurricane of October 1987 I came to check the set with a feeling of impending doom. The roads were blocked with the fallen trees and when I got to Elstree the security guards told me the damage was pretty bad. Expecting the worst, I approached the set to discover that luckily it was virtually untouched by the violent storms - the security guards had been having me on."

Opposite: **Rita Simons (Roxy Mitchell) and Samantha Janus (Ronnie Mitchell) filming *EastEnders* on location in Weymouth, Dorset.**

The Albert Square houses actually have no backs as the interior shots are filmed at an adjacent studio. When the set was first built it had just three sides and Bridge Street but over the years various buildings have been added including the bookies, Beale's Plaice, George Street and Walford East Tube Station.

EastEnders is a working set, so the BBC can't accommodate visitors, but *EastEnders* fans can visit various locations used on the programme which aren't inside Elstree Studios. For example, Den Watts was shot by the side of the Grand Union Canal, near Water Road, London NW10, Lofty and Michelle's marriage was filmed at the chapel in the grounds of Shenley Hospital, Shenley in Hertfordshire and Charlie Cotton's funeral, which coincided with the blessing of Ricky and Sam's marriage, was filmed at St Nicholas' Church, Elstree Hill, but most church scenes set in Walford are filmed at St Andrew's Church, Watford.

Pauline Fowler's and Frank Butcher's funerals were filmed at Hendon Crematorium in north London, Windsor Racecourse was used for scenes featuring Alfie and Kat, and Den's funeral took place at North Watford Cemetery, where a fake gravestone was put in place showing that Den was buried in the same grave as Angie. Walford's Register Office is usually Watford or Hendon Town Hall and if a court scene is required the location is in St Albans or Hatfield.

Over the years some episodes of *EastEnders* have been filmed abroad, in Amsterdam, Paris, Venice, Ireland, Normandy in France, Portugal and Marbella and Torremolinos in Spain and many scenes have been filmed in different parts of the UK including Blackpool, Manchester, Brighton, Portsmouth, Nottingham and Weymouth.

By the spring of 2008 there was talk that a new identical Albert Square might be built 28 miles away at Pinewood Studios as the current set was not suitable for High Definition (HD) filming as it would show too many scenery defects like cracks, chips and patching. So far this has yet to happen.

Sat nav references:

Elstree Studios (WD6 1JG)

Hendon (NW4 4BG)

Hendon Crematorium (NW7 1NB)

North Watford Cemetery (WD25 0AW)

St Andrew's Church (WD17 4PY)

Watford Town Hall (WD17 3EX)

Windsor Racecourse (SL4 5JJ)

Holby City

Borehamwood

Despite being a spin-off of *Casualty* and supposedly set in the same fictional hospital, *Holby City* is filmed nowhere near Bristol where *Casualty* was filmed until its recent move to Cardiff. It is actually shot entirely on a purpose-built set at Elstree Studios in Borehamwood, Hertfordshire, also home to *EastEnders*. An office block used by BBC staff is used as one of the hospital's entrances.

Occasionally, characters and storylines of the two series overlap and sometimes characters in one refer to a ward in another, but generally, the two series have separate identities.

Sat nav reference:

Elstree Studios (WD6 1JG)

Goodnight Sweetheart

Above : **The Royal Oak which played the wartime pub in** *Goodnight Sweetheart.*

Sat nav reference:

Royal Oak (E2 7RG)

The BBC comedy series *Goodnight Sweetheart* stars Nicholas Lyndhurst as Gary Sparrow, the man who juggled two women in different time zones, one modern day and the other during the Second World War. Unlike *Doctor Who*, we never saw how Gary manages to travel in time, he simply walked down a passageway off a London street and switches time. The passageway, Ducketts Passage, where he walks was actually Ezra Street near the flower market off Columbia Road, Bethnal Green.

His 1940s wife Phoebe, played by Liz Carling, runs a pub The Royal Oak, and its exterior was played by the real-life Royal Oak at 73 Columbia Road. The pub has also been featured in the film *Lock, Stock and Two Smoking Barrels*, the BBC series *The Hello Girls* and ex-*Eastenders* star Barbara Windsor popped in during her appearance in the BBC genealogy show *Who Do You Think You Are?* as her grandfather used to drink there. The modern day exterior of Gary's wartime memorabilia shop Blitz and Pieces was in nearby Old Street and the interior was a studio set. For more details go to: www.royaloaklondon.com

London's Burning

Above: **Dockhead Fire Station the setting for** *London's Burning.*

Real life Dockhead Fire Station was used as the fictional Blackwall Station in the long-runnning ITV drama series *London's Burning* and played home to the Blue Watch crew. For the original 1986 90-minute *London's Burning* film, from which the series began, the whole of the Dockhead was used for filming. Makers London Weekend Television had full cooperation from the London Fire Brigade and the production team put portable cabins in the station yard for the real fire-fighters to use for the six-week duration of filming.

The cabins were used to replace the fire-fighters' relaxation area, the canteen, the mess and sleeping quarters while they were used for filming. In exchange for allowing their mess area to be used firefighters were given free meals on the catering bus. When a full series was commissioned, the production team built a full scale replica of the upper floor of Dockhead at Long Lane Studios in London. All exterior shots at Dockhead used the yard and the appliance bay. Because Dockhead was a busy working fire station (although it is currently due to be demolished and then rebuilt) the first priority of the film team was to make sure they were never in the way when the real fire-fighters headed out on a 'shout'. For the last two series filming switched to Leyton Fire Station in Leyton, east London.

Silk

First screened on BBC One in 2011, this six-part drama follows a group of barristers in fictional Shoe Lane Chambers as two of them – Martha Costello (played by Maxine Peake) and her rival Clive Reader (Rupert Penry-Jones) - vie to become a Queen's Counsel or 'take silk' as it is known.

The series was penned by writer Peter Moffat who said he based it on his own experiences at the Bar and as such, it was filmed almost entirely around actual chambers and court houses which adds to its authenticity. The main location which played the exterior of the legal chambers was Goldsmith Chambers, a real barristers' chambers in Temple in the City of London.

"We had to approach the barristers' chambers which rent the building off the Middle Temple and ask if we could film exteriors there which we did," said Location Manager Rupert Bray. "Then we built an interior in an old hunting lodge in Mill Hill which was a convent for a time but the nuns moved out and sold it to a developer. We managed to nip in there and as *Silk* has been recommissioned, we may be able to go back."

As avid viewers will know, Martha's flat pops up several times in the series but finding a suitable location didn't prove easy. The production snapped up what they thought was an ideal basement flat in which to film in Notting Hill but were eventually asked to leave after two visits.

"The residents of Notting Hill don't really like filming and a few people made life very difficult," Rupert revealed. "Although the flat we were shooting in had access to a communal garden, they didn't want us to use it. Even though I offered to make a charity donation to the garden committee, they flatly refused to allow us to put lights outside the window or cables in the garden. It just proved too difficult to service in the end so we then found another privately owned flat in St Andrews Square in Surbiton in Surrey."

As fans of *Silk* will recognise, the majority of scenes were shot in the Temple area, pretty much the same location in which popular legal drama *Kavanagh QC* was filmed in the 90s (and also used for *Pirates of the Caribbean: On Stranger Tides)*. Nearby are the Royal Courts of Justice on the Strand where Martha, a criminal lawyer, appeals on a number of occasions.

Other courts used in the series are Kingston Crown Court which is currently in use and a real coup for the production who were allowed in during the working week, the old Crown Court in Kingston which is disused and the closed Magistrates Courts' at Dorking and at Shoreditch. "It's just a case of finding the right court," continued Rupert. "You can film at real courts at the weekend apart from the Old Bailey and certain criminal courts. The trouble is if you need more than one or two days you're stuck as they're then in session. So we were lucky as we managed to get in and out quickly and have access when we needed it."

Other locations to spot include all the pubs around Middle Temple which are normally closed at weekends, outfitters in the Temple (from where Martha's Pupil steals a wig) and the old Bird's Eye headquarters, Walton Court in Walton.

Sat nav references:

Goldsmith Chambers (EC4Y 7BL)

Kingston Crown Court (KT1 2BB)

Magistrates Court at Dorking (RH4 1SX)

Spooks

London

The first series of this long-running spy drama was screened by the BBC in 2002 and became an instant hit, going on to win a BAFTA. Set among a team of M15 intelligence officers (who are nicknamed 'spooks', hence the series' title) at Thames House in London the series has seen them battle all kinds of threats to the UK's national security from Al Qaeda to more home grown threats.

Peter Firth, Matthew MacFadyen, Keeley Hawes, David Oyelowo and Jenny Agutter starred in the initial six-part series and since then a host of famous faces have featured in the show including Rupert Penry-Jones, Nicola Walker, Richard Armitage, Hermione Norris, Max Brown and Sophia Myles.

Right: **Jo Portman (Miranda Raison) and Adam Carter (Rupert Penry-Jones) go into action in a dramatic scene in** *Spooks*. *Opposite page (top):* **Freemason's Hall in Great Queen Street, London which plays Thames House in** *Spooks*.

Freemason's Hall in Great Queen Street, London which is home to the United Grand Lodge of England, doubles up as the exterior of Thames House, while the majority of internal shots in the 'Grid' where the team work together on their latest mission, are filmed on a specially constructed set on an industrial estate in Bermondsey, south east London. Interior scenes had previously been filmed at a former university building in west London and then at Pinewood Studios. The design of the Grid is based exactly on the interior of the real

Thames House. Over the years, *Spooks* has been filmed across most of London and has spilt over into surrounding counties such as Kent and Surrey where for instance, an old Ministry of Defence complex near Chertsey, doubled up as an American air force base. In another episode, a manor house in the same grounds was used as a secret hiding location for some of the characters.

Shooting in the heart of London with its huge, busy population of people and traffic is never easy but Location Manager Thomas Elgood who worked on some episodes of the show said going the extra mile to obtain a certain look is exactly what makes *Spooks* so eminently watchable. "Filming in London is a struggle and for scenes to work you need plenty of space but *Spooks* is very popular and fortunately, people are often willing to help when asked," he said. "We take great care to get all the relevant permission from various people like Westminster Council, the police and the Royal Parks who are particularly good and geared up for filming. When you see the finished version, you're always glad you made the effort to get the permission because it's worth it."

Fans of the show may recall a major explosion at a central London hotel in one series. This was in fact staged inside Wandsworth Town Hall, while the exteriors were of the Adelphi Building close to the Strand. Incidentally, there's a small street nearby which often stands in for 10 Downing Street in various television productions. Other central London locations include Forbes House in Halkin Street, Belgravia, which played as the Iranian Embassy. With its grand exterior it is perfect as the Embassy's stately entrance. Several scenes were shot all around the Albert Memorial, the Royal Albert Hall and St James Park thanks to friendly assistance from the Royal Parks which welcomes television crews.

Further into the city at Moorgate, a sniper in one episode is seen taking aim from a tall building within City Point. And while viewers may think they're watching certain scenes in the heart of London, they may actually have been filmed around the Old Naval College in Greenwich which with its tall Victorian buildings and pillars was perfect as the grandeur of the West End, particularly Whitehall. Clearly, in an on-going series such as *Spooks*, more and more locations are added every season and sometimes studios are required to film particular scenes. For instance, in series five, the final episode was shot at Action Underwater Studios in Basildon which required Adam Carter (played by Rupert Penry-Jones) and Ros Myers (Hermione Norris) to spend a great deal of time immersed in water.

Sat nav references:

Action Underwater Studios (SS13 1DW)

Forbes House (SW1X 7DS)

Freemason's Hall (WC2B 5AZ)

Old Naval College (SE10 9LW)

Royal Albert Hall (SW7 2AP)

Wandsworth Town Hall (SW18 2PU)

2008 saw filming start on a *Spooks* spin-off series *Spooks: Code 9*. Set in 2013, London had been evacuated after a nuclear attack and M15 has moved in to set up field offices across the UK. Former Bradford police station The Tyrls was used for production and filming and many scenes were shot on location across Bradford and Leeds.

Also in London

Sat nav reference:

Bridge Cafe (W3 0AP)

Sat nav reference:

Hornsey Town Hall (N8 9JJ)

Sat nav reference:

House of Fraser (EC4N 7HR)

Sat nav references:

Newburgh Road (W3 6DQ)

Standard Road (NW10 6EX)

The Apprentice

The Bridge Cafe in West Acton, London has seen a boost in business since it's been used as the location where the losing team in *The Apprentice* are sent to deliberate. Frank and Jerry Marcangelo are thrilled that the publicity of the show has given their long standing cafe more business. "I think they picked this one out because it's a working man's cafe and it's their punishment that they have to come here!" joked Frank. "It's definitely helped business - lots of tourists come here before they go up to London." The cafe, in Westfields Road, Acton, London, is open from 6.30am on weekdays so does a big business in breakfast although *The Apprentice* candidates only get a drink while they are there, usually served by Frank. "I give them the drinks so I've been seen on TV a couple of times," added Frank.

The Hour

The BBC drama *The Hour*, which stars Romola Garai, Dominic West and Ben Whishaw, takes viewers behind the scenes of the launch of a topical news programme in London 1956. The drama, written and created by Bafta award-winning Abi Morgan, was mainly filmed at Hornsey Town Hall, an art deco former council building in Crouch End, North London. Hornsey Town Hall, which was used by Hornsey Borough Council as its headquarters until 1966 is Grade II* which meant it was perfect for filming as most of its period features were intact.

Love Soup

David Renwick's inventive comedy drama *Love Soup* starred Tamsin Greig as department store cosmetic counter manager Alice Chenery, whose struggle to find the perfect partner leads her down a path of disastrous dates and embarrassing mishaps. If the department store used for filming looked real, it's because it was - it's actually House of Fraser's City branch, 68 King William Street. Because it is the City of London branch, it isn't open at weekends which meant that in addition to exterior shots, the interior scenes could also be filmed there. Before she moved to London, Alice lived in Brighton and the building used to house her flat was the attractive 1930s Furze Croft apartment block in Furze Hill.

Minder

Even Arthur Daley was conned every time he went into the Winchester Club - because it was actually a studio set. But it wasn't always. In some early episodes of the popular ITV series about the exploits of dodgy dealing Arthur Daley, an actual drinking club in Chalk Farm, north London, situated next to the tube station was used. The outside door to the Winchester Club actually belonged to a building at 2b Newburgh Road, Acton, north London - but characters are never actually seen going through it because it led into a private flat. Arthur's car lot changed location over the years but the one last used by the *Minder* production team was at 89 Churchfield Road, Acton. Arthur's lock-up, where he keeps all his dodgy gear, had changed since *Minder* began. For the last series it was at the rear of 7, Standard Road in north London. The pier that Arthur and Ray were always seen walking down during *Minder's* title sequence - that was Southend Pier in Essex.

'Allo, 'Allo
Dad's Army
Kingdom
Little Britain
Lovejoy
Martin Chuzzlewit
The Mill on the Floss

'Allo, 'Allo

Lynford

The BBC found the ideal location to play wartime France in 'Allo, 'Allo, the popular comedy about the French resistance fighters. For Lynford Hall, at Lynford in Norfolk was designed in the neo-Gothic style along the lines of a French Chateau. It was ideal and saved the BBC the expense of

using a real French location. Lynford Hall was perfect for 'Allo, 'Allo as the front of the main part of the building was ideal to play Gestapo officer Herr Flick's headquarters and because the cobbled courtyard round the back was easily turned into fictional Novienne square, including Café Rene. The BBC production team built the front of the Café and other Novienne shops over the front of the archways. Interiors were filmed in a studio. Lynford Hall is now a hotel and conference centre and has a licence for civil marriages. Further details are available at www.lynfordhallhotel.co.uk

Right: **French-style country house Lynford Hall - home to Cafe Rene and Herr Flick in 'Allo, 'Allo.**

Sat nav reference:

Lynford Hall (IP26 5HW)

Dad's Army

Thetford

A German invasion force would have been completely foiled if it had tried to find Walmington-on-Sea, where Captain Mainwaring led his Home Guard Platoon in the BBC comedy *Dad's Army*. For Walmington-on-Sea was supposed to be a small town on the coast in Sussex. Yet the whole series was filmed in and around the Norfolk town of Thetford. Producers were lucky from the start because the MoD allowed them to use the Stanford Battle Area, a large nearby

Right: **They don't like it up 'em...the Walmington-on-Sea platoon charge.**

training area requisitioned by the army during the war. It was used for many scenes including the show's iconic closing credits.

Bill Pertwee, who played Air Raid Warden Hodges, said: "We used it for a tremendous amount of locations, basically anything that involved chasing across fields like the episode with the barrage balloon, *The Day The Balloon Went Up*." The cast and crew used to stay at the Bell Hotel and at the Anchor Hotel in Thetford. The streets of the town were used for filming and The Guildhall which doubled as Walmington Town Hall in the episodes *The Captain's Car* and *Time on my Hands*. Much of the town was used including the Almshouses in Old Bury Road, which appeared in *The Face on the Poster*, Mill Lane, where the platoon march in *The Deadly Attachment* and Nether Row, which appeared in four episodes: *The Armoured Might of Lance Corporal Jones*, *Man Hunt*, *The Big Parade* and *Time on My Hands*.

Above: **Captain Mainwaring (Arthur Lowe) and the vicar (Frank Williams) outside the Guildhall.**

Thetford's Palace Cinema (now a bingo hall) featured in both *The Big Parade* and *A Soldier's Farewell*. Old Bury Road featured in *The Face on the Poster* and Mill Lane was used as the road to the harbour in the episode *The Deadly Attachment*.

The pier at Great Yarmouth was used for the episode *Menace From The Deep*, and a disused airfield near Diss was also utilised. Sheringham railway station which is now on a preserved line and part of North Norfolk Railway, was used for an episode called *The Royal Train*. The Norfolk Broads were used for an episode *Sons of the Sea*.

Another memorable episode, *The Two and a Half Feathers*, which saw the whole cast playing out a long desert scene, was filmed at large sandpits at Kings Lynn. Drinkstone Mill at Drinkstone, Suffolk was used for the episode *Don't Forget the Diver* and not far away is Wacton, setting for the episode *Round and Round Went The Big Wheel*.

Santon Downham was the site of the bridge used in *Brain Versus Brawn* and Brandon Station was the railway station used in *The Big Parade*. A National Trust castle, Oxburgh Hall, was used as Peabody Museum in *Museum Piece*. Kilverstone doubled up as Waterloo in *A Soldier's Farewell* where Captain Mainwaring dreams he is Napoleon.

Lynford Hall was used as the backdrop to the shooting range in *Wake Up Walmington*, an episode which also featured the Six Bells, a pub in Bardwell, which reappeared in the episode *Ring Dem Bells*.

Not strictly a television location, but one of interest to fans of *Dad's Army* is the pretty village of Chalfont St Giles in Buckinghamshire, which was used as the setting for the excellent 1971 *Dad's Army* feature film. Members of The Dad's Army Appreciation Society have staged tours of all these locations. For details see: www.dadsarmy.co.uk. See also: www.explorethetford.co.uk

Sat nav references:

Drinkstone Mill (IP30 9SP)

The Guildhall (IP24 2DS)

Oxburgh Hall (PE33 9PS)

Palace Cinema (IP24 2DT)

Sheringham Station (NR26 8RA)

The Six Bells (IP31 1AW)

Kingdom

Swaffham

Above: **Stephen Fry plays Peter Kingdom and is seen here on location in Swaffham.**

The real life market town of Swaffham in Norfolk doubled as Market Shipborough in ITV1's popular comedy drama *Kingdom* which ran for three series from 2007 to 2009.

Stephen Fry starred as a country solicitor, Peter Kingdom, who set more store by human concerns than the law. Hermione Norris played his batty, man-eating sister Beatrice alongside a strong supporting cast which included Celia Imrie, Phyllida Law and Tony Slattery.

Stephen has actually lived a few miles outside Swaffham for many years and was delighted when the decision was taken to film in beautiful Norfolk. "When we decided on making *Kingdom*, I was very sure that the producers and writers should visit Swaffham and perhaps gain some inspiration from it," he said at the time.

"I had secretly hoped that they would be so struck by the town that they would want to film there. All of us connected to *Kingdom* are grateful to the town and its hospitable people for allowing us the opportunity to make the series there."

Although Market Shipborough was supposedly a coastal town, Swaffham is miles from the sea but a soundtrack cleverly gives the impression otherwise. Scenes of the quayside and the harbour were filmed at Wells-next-the-Sea in north Norfolk while Holkham was used for beach shots. Viewers watching repeats will note that they feature in the programme's opening credits.

Kingdom fans visiting Swaffham will have no trouble spotting landmarks featured heavily in the series, particularly the town centre. The market place is a familiar sight as is Oakleigh House which played as Kingdom's office. The Market Shipborough sign actually covered up the real Swaffham town

Above (left): **Oakleigh House, Swaffham, which played Peter Kingdom's office** *(centre)* **St Peter's and St Paul's Church which appeared in** *Kingdom* *(right)* **the cast on location.**

Sat nav references:

Break Charity Shop (PE37 7AB)

Cockley Cley Hall (PE37 8AG)

Doves of Swaffham (PE37 7LA)

Greyhound Pub (PE37 7AQ)

Newmarket Racecourse (CB8 0TF)

Oakleigh House (PE37 7QH)

Queens College, Cambridge University (CB3 9ET)

Swaffham Library (PE37 7DF)

Swaffham Museum (PE37 7DQ)

sign during filming, while the town's Greyhound Pub doubled as The Startled Duck in the show.

Both Swaffham Methodist Church and St Peters and St Pauls Church featured as Market Shipborough's local church while Swaffham's Church Rooms became Market Shipborough's Church Rooms. Swaffham Library also popped up as the local library.

Even some of the local shops got in on the action with a Break Charity Shop transformed into Tiger Lily's Sex Shop in one episode! Doves of Swaffham became a ladies clothes shop in another.

Other locations used included Swaffham Museum; Happisburgh village, beach and cliffs; Denver Sluice in Kings Lynn, Norfolk and RAF Marham in Norfolk, which became RAF Fakenheath for two days for a storyline in which Kingdom investigates an American soldier serving in the US Air Force. Cockley Cley Hall doubled up as Aunt Auriel's house; racecourse scenes were shot at the famous Newmarket Racecourse and Queens College, Cambridge University appeared as Peter Kingdom's old college.

Little Britain

Southwold

Old Haven, Darkley Noone, Troby, Sneddy, Herby and, of course, Llanddewi Brefi – they're the places where the weird and wonderful characters in the television comedy series *Little Britain* like Emily and Florence, Vicky Pollard, Lou and Andy, Dennis Waterman and Jeremy Rent, Kenny Craig and Daffyd live.

And before you think that the hit show's writers and stars David Walliams and Matt Lucas have invented names that are too wacky to be believable, keep reading – for the following six names are real places in Britain: Bozomzeal (in Devon), Blubberhouses (Yorkshire), Clenchwarton (Norfolk), Dull (Perthshire), Pratt's Bottom (Greater London) and Ugley (Essex).

For series two of *Little Britain* Old Haven, home to those would-be ladies Emily Howard and Florence, was actually picturesque Southwold in Suffolk. Producer Geoff Posner told the local paper The East Anglian Daily Times: "It's perfect for Emily and Florence, the failed transvestites, who have a somewhat Victorian air about them - like Southwold!"

For the third series Eastbourne, east Sussex played the town and holiday makers out for a stroll were faced with two men dressed as women enjoying a ride on a carousel and the sight of Matt Lucas dressed as a baby. This time Posner told Eastbourne Today newspaper: "The characters Emily and Florence live in a Victorian world and the architecture of Eastbourne fits their world completely."

Scenes supposed to be Troby, where Lou and Andy live, have been filmed in various locations. For the third series a scene where Andy hopped out of his wheelchair and joined in a rugby match when Lou wasn't watching was filmed at London Skolars New River Stadium in White Hart Lane, London. Another sketch, when Andy did a parachute jump, was filmed at RAF Hendon, north London. Other scenes were shot in Notting Hill, London.

Above: **David Walliams and Matt Lucas film scenes from *Little Britain*.**
Top: **Emily (David Walliams) and Florence (Matt Lucas) enjoying a carousel in Eastbourne.**

Scenes of Lou and Andy's home have been filmed on the Cranbrook Estate in Bethnal Green, London and the scene where Andy bought a snake was shot at a real pet shop, Magri's Pets at 205 Roman Road, also in Bethnal Green. Bubbles Devere kept that fabulous shape by spending lots of time at Hill Grange Health Spa in Trump, scenes for which were filmed at Gaddesden Place in Hemel Hempstead, headquarters of computer software company Xara. Gaddesden Place is a veteran location and has been in many films and television series including *Sharpe, Jeeves and Wooster, Jonathan Creek*, Lewis and *Foyle's War*.

The very striking former Royal Masonic School building in Bushey, Hertfordshire was used as Kelsey Grammar School, where Mr Cleaves taught. It has also been used many times for films including *The Meaning of Life* and on television for *Inspector Morse, Hex* and *My Dad's The Prime Minister*. The building is now being converted into luxury apartments. Daffyd's village of Llandewi Breffi is spelt differently from the real village of Llanddewi Brefi (which has only one 'f') in west Wales. There have been reports of attempted theft of village signs even though no scenes have actually been filmed there.

Sat nav references:

Gaddesden Place (HP2 6EX)

Magri's Pets (E2 0QY)

New River Stadium (N22 5QW)

Lovejoy

Long Melford

Above (left): **Belchamp Hall, which played Lady Jane's home** *(right)* **Ian McShane as** *Lovejoy.*

You might not bump into that loveable rogue *Lovejoy* if you head to Long Melford in Suffolk but you will find scores of genuine antique shops full of the sort of stuff Lovejoy would love to get his hands on. Long Melford, so named because of its particularly long high street, which is three miles long, was one of around a dozen in Suffolk regularly used for filming *Lovejoy*, the highly successful BBC series which stars Ian McShane as the eponymous antique dealer.

The attractive 16th Century Bull Hotel was regularly featured in the series along with many of the village's antique shops including Neptune Antiques and Ringer's Yard.

Over at Belchamp Walter, opposite the beautiful 15th Century village church with medieval wall paintings, is Belchamp Hall, an elegant Queen Anne redbrick house, which was used as Lady Jane's home, Felsham Hall, in the series. The Hall is also available for hire for conferences, weddings and parties and the converted stables can be rented for holidays and short breaks. For more details go to www.belchamphall.com The attractive 300-year-old thatched Half Moon pub at nearby Belchamp St Paul was a familiar sight in the Autumn 1993 series of *Lovejoy* when it became one of his locals. Elsewhere many other towns and villages in the area were regularly used in the series including Braintree, Hadleigh, Kersey, Lavenham, Felsham, Sudbury, Halstead, Bildeston and Bury St Edmunds.

Sat nav references:

Belchamp Hall (CO10 7AT)

Half Moon pub (CO10 7DP)

Martin Chuzzlewit

King's Lynn

Written in 1843, *Martin Chuzzlewit* was Charles Dickens' sixth novel, and filming requirements called for a labyrinth of tiny streets, supposedly in early 19th Century London. The BBC found the perfect location in the attractive Norfolk town of King's Lynn. The story centres on an inheritance and the contrasting destinies of the wealthy brothers Chuzzlewit and featured an all-star cast including Sir John Mills, Paul Schofield, Keith Allen, Tom Wilkinson and Julia Sawalha.

King's Lynn was one of England's foremost ports as early as the 12th Century and even today late medieval merchants' houses stretch back to the river between cobbled lanes and the famous Custom House. Those tiny streets proved to be perfect for the production team and where there

Above: **Peckover House in Cambridgeshire played Montague Tigg's home.**

were modern road markings mud was used cover them up. King's Lynn Council's offices doubled as Mrs Todgers' boarding houses and the frontages of cottages at King's Straithe, which also played early New York in the film *Revolution*, were used extensively. St Margaret's House and the lane next door appeared, as did the back of King's Street. "King's Lynn offered us the labyrinth of tiny streets that Dickens mentions in the novel," said Production Designer Gavin Davies. "I could get seven important locations within 10 minutes of one another."

Elsewhere, The Fleece Inn, a 14th Century pub in the Worcestershire Village of Bretforton, appeared as The Blue Dragon and a National Trust property, Peckover House in Cambridgeshire, played Montague Tigg's home. See www.nationaltrust.org.uk for further details. Honington Hall, a 17th Century house at Shipston-on-Stour, Warwickshire, also appeared. The house, which has also featured in *Our Mutual Friend* and *Keeping Up Appearances*, is open to the public at certain times. For further details telephone: 01608 661434.

The Mill on the Floss

Bintree

Above: **Bintree Mill, the main setting for *The Mill on the Floss*.**

The BBC's 1997 adaptation of *The Mill on the Floss*, George Eliot's classic tale of unrequited love which stars Emily Watson, James Frain and Bernard Hill, who went on to play Captain Smith in the blockbuster film Titanic, featured a number of stunning locations. To find the principal location, that of the Dorlcote Mill, Location Manager Jeremy Johns visited 50 water-mills all over the country from Devon to the Lake District and from Wales to East Anglia.

"When we found most of the film's other settings and locations in the vicinity, Bintree was a winner," said Jeremy. The interiors of Dorlcote – the corn-loft, milling-floor and sack chute – were found in another mill 16 miles away in Burgh-next-Aylsham and the kitchen and parlour interiors were filmed in an old farmhouse in Salle. Nearby were the locations for Lawyer Wakem's house and Lucy Deane's house, while the flood and rowing scenes were shot on a lake near Bintree.

Also in East Anglia

Hi-De-Hi

The BBC comedy *Hi-De-Hi*, set in a 1950s holiday camp, was another huge hit from the script-writing partnership of Jimmy Perry and David Croft. It was popular with the public but holiday giants Butlins were less than impressed and refused to let the BBC use one of their holiday camps for filming.

Another company, Warners, had no such objections to the show and allowed the BBC to film at their holiday camp at Dovercourt, near Frinton-on-Sea. Sadly it was bulldozed several years ago to make way for a housing estate, although there is a section for touring caravans at the nearby Dovercourt Caravan Park.

The Midlands

By The Sword Divided

Market Harborough

Above: **Stunning Rockingham Castle, still owned by the same family for nearly 500 years.**

Location managers could hardly have found a better location than Rockingham Castle for the BBC's 1983-1985 series *By The Sword Divided*. Set in 1640 during the English Civil War, the series followed the lives of the Royalist Lacey family and documents their involvement in the conflict. It starred Julian Glover as Sir Martin Lacey, Sharon Maughan as his daughter Anne Lacey, and Timothy Bentinck, famous on radio as David Archer in *The Archers*, as his son Tom Lacey, and ran for two 10-part series.

Rockingham was perfect as Arnescote and has been in the Watson family since 1530. The first Lord Rockingham, Sir Lewis Watson, was a Royalist, but his wife Eleanor was a Parliamentarian. The property has had real-life experiences of the Civil War when it was badly damaged.

More than three centuries after the Civil War, Rockingham, which is still owned by the Watson family, saw Cavalier and Roundhead battles again when the BBC arrived. Rockingham Castle, which is licenced for civil weddings, is open to the public throughout the summer on certain days of the week. See www.rockinghamcastle.com for details.

Sat nav reference:

Rockingham Castle (LE16 8TH)

Dangerfield

Warwick

Right: **Lord Leycester Hospital in Warwick, the town where the BBC drama *Dangerfield* was filmed.**

The BBC drama, which starred Nigel Havers as police surgeon Dr Jonathan Paige and Jane Gurnett as Detective Inspector Gillian Cramer ran between 1995 and 1999 and was filmed in and around the beautiful town of Warwick, dominated by magnificent Warwick Castle. The key location for the show was Dr Paige's surgery and if it looked authentic that was because it was, as the exterior scenes were filmed at a real-life surgery, The Old Dispensary in Castle Street, Warwick.

The first four series of the show featured Nigel Le Vaillant as Dr Paul Dangerfield and his home for the first three series was played by a house on Shipston Road near Stratford Upon Avon. For series four he moved to another house, played by The Malt House in Mill Street, Warwick. The house that played Dr Paige's home is in Castle Street, Warwick. For the first four series the real life police stations at Leamington Spa and Warwick doubled as the police station. St Mary's Church in the centre of Warwick was used for the wedding of Dr Dangerfield's daughter Alison.

Sat nav references:

The Malt House (CV34 4HB)

The Old Dispensary (CV34 4BP)

St Mary's Church (CV34 4RA)

Inspector Morse

Oxford

Above: **Beautiful rooftop view of All Souls College.**

There is very little of central Oxford that didn't, at some time, appear in *Inspector Morse*, the award-winning detective series which starred the late John Thaw as the thoughtful Oxford sleuth. Some landmarks are easily recognisable from the television, but others, notably the colleges, are more difficult because often several different real locations were used to make one fictional place.

The King's Arms, known as the KA, on the corner of Holywell Street and Parks Road, is one of the easily identifiable places - and was used by Morse to down a few pints of his favourite Samuel Smith's best bitter in several episodes. Just along in Holywell Street is the Music Room, owned by Wadham College, which was used in the 1993 episode *Twilight of the Gods* when opera singer Gladys Probert, played by the late Sheila Gish, gave a masterclass.

Back in Broad Street is the bookshop, Blackwells, where Morse was seen in several episodes buying books, and next door is the White Horse pub, another location where Morse could often be found drinking. On the other side of Broad Street is the impressive Sheldonian Theatre, where Oxford University confers its degrees. In Inspector Morse it was used in the episode *Dead on Time* when Morse took his ex-fiancée Susan Fallon to a concert there.

Above: **John Thaw and Kevin Whately pictured outside the imposing Radcliffe Camera, Oxford.**

To the side of the Sheldonian Theatre, next door to the Bodleian Library lies the square used for *Twilight of The Gods* where a shooting took place. In Radcliffe Square, not far from Broad Street, is the unusually shaped Radcliffe Camera and next door to it is Brasenose College which appeared as two fictional colleges Beaufort and Beaumont in various episodes.

Seen from the beautiful Christchurch meadow is Merton College which appeared in the episode *The Infernal Serpent*. Christchurch itself was used as the backdrop to several episodes, and is very noticeable because of its distinctive Tom Tower. The porter's lodge at Pembroke College was used for the episode *Deceived By Flight* when Sergeant Robbie Lewis (Kevin Whately) posed as a porter to catch a murderer and a smuggler. "I think we filmed at every college in Oxford that would have us," said Location Manager Russell Lodge. "And that was 90 per cent of them."

Out of the city at Wolvercote is the delightful Trout pub on the bank of the River Isis. It is from the bridge next to the pub that Morse and Lewis watched a frogman recover the Anglo-Saxon belt buckle, the Wolvercote Tongue, in the episode of the same name. The Randolph Hotel in Beaumont Street also featured heavily in the episode and also appeared in other stories. It was also regularly used by John Thaw when he stayed in Oxford for filming and appeared in the film *Shadowlands*. Oxford isn't the only place used to film Morse though and in the episode Masonic Mysteries none of the city was used. Although on screen it looks like Morse rarely leaves Oxford, usually only five days of filming out of 25 were done in the city, with the rest of the days shot in other locations doubling as Oxford.

Above: **An aerial view of Magdalen College and Bridge.**

A territorial army centre in Southall, London, was used as the police station for the first two series, although for those series the front we saw on screen was the front of the real Oxford police station. For the third, fourth and fifth series a TA centre in Harrow played the police station and a Ministry of Defence laboratory in Harefield in Hertfordshire did the same job in the sixth and seventh series, but was demolished in the spring of 1993.

The front of the police station was not shown that much on screen as Morse and Lewis mainly use the back entrance. Morse's home was actually miles from Oxford. It was a ground floor flat in a Victorian block in Castlebar Road, Ealing. When Morse's home caught fire in one episode a set of the flat was built in a studio and burned, although fake smoke came through a broken window at the actual flat too. It was filmed in Ealing because it was cheaper not to travel to Oxford as it didn't involve an expensive overnight stay for the actors and crew. Many of the streets in Ealing look very similar to houses on the Woodstock or Banbury roads out of Oxford.

Stately homes were also often prominent in *Morse* including Cornbury Park in Charlbury, Oxfordshire, which was used for the episode *Greeks Bearing Gifts*, Englefield House, near Reading, which had also been used for *Jeeves and Wooster* and the mini-series *A Woman of Substance*, appeared in *Twilight of The Gods* and 14th Century Shirburn Castle was used for the 1994 episode *Happy Families.*

Another of Morse's favourite pubs, which is supposed to be near Oxford, was actually filmed at The Crown at Bray in Berkshire. "We used the inside a lot," said Russell Lodge. "We slightly decorated the inside by changing the pictures, and they are still up now." The pub was picked because the *Morse* production team were filming at nearby Bray film studios. The 1998 episode *The Wench Is Dead,* which saw actor Matthew Finney join Morse as his new sidekick Adrian Kershaw instead of Lewis, was filmed at The Black Country Museum at Dudley and on canals in Northamptonshire and Wiltshire.

The graveyard scenes – supposedly in Ireland – were filmed at Abersoch in Wales and a few extra fibreglass gravestones were added to real ones there. Morse spent most of the episode in Radcliffe Infirmary in Oxford and the scenes of him leaving were actually filmed there. The Radcliffe appears again in the final episode of *Inspector Morse*, *The Remorseful Day*, which was first broadcast on November 15th 2000, as does the Randolph Hotel for a scene where Morse had coffee with Dr Harrison. Morse and Lewis met for their last pint at the Victoria Arms in Mill Lane Old Marston and at the end of the episode Morse collapsed and died of a heart attack in the quadrangle of Exeter College in Turl Street.

Sat nav references:

The Black Country Museum (DY1 4SQ)

Blackwells (OX1 3BQ)

Brasenose College (OX1 4AJ)

Cornbury Park (OX7 3EH)

The Crown (SL6 2AH)

Englefield House (RG7 5DU)

Exeter College (OX1 3DP)

The King's Arms (OX1 3SP)

Pembroke College (CB2 1RF)

The Randolph Hotel (OX1 2LN)

Sheldonian Theatre (OX1 3AZ)

Trout pub (SN7 8RF)

Victoria Arms (OX3 0PZ)

Wadham College (OX1 3PN)

White Horse pub (OX1 3BB)

Keeping Up Appearances

Coventry

The Coventry suburb of Binley Woods was the fictional home of social-climbing Hyacinth Bucket (or Bouquet as she pronounces it) and her put upon husband Richard, in the hit BBC comedy series *Keeping Up Appearances*. The owners of 117 Heather Road, which doubled up as the exterior of the Bucket residence, thought it was a joke when a location manager first asked if the BBC could use the house for filming as they did not know that their neighbours at Number 119 had already agreed to let the BBC use their home as the Bucket's neighbours Elizabeth and Emmet's house.

Before filming began the production team used to put a fake garden at the side of the garage, extra plants in the existing flower border and add extra net curtains so the occupants couldn't be seen during filming outside. Patricia Routledge, who played Hyacinth, used the house's dining room as her make-up room but the interior scenes were filmed later at BBC studios. A few miles away, on a council estate in the Stoke district of Coventry, is Michell Close where Number Three played the home of Hyacinth's brother Onslow and his wife Daisy. The house was chosen because there is a scrapyard at the end of the road which was used as Onslow's yard.

Sat nav references:

Heather Road (CV3 2DB)

Michell Close (CV3 1DG)

Lewis

Oxford

Right: **Laurence Fox as Detective Sergeant James Hathaway and Kevin Whately as Detective Inspector Robert Lewis, the stars of *Lewis*.**

Not even Kevin Whately who plays the unsophisticated Lewis believed he'd ever reprise the role he played for 13 years as *Morse's* sidekick in ITV's popular police drama *Inspector Morse*. After the death of Morse and of course his alter ego, the late John Thaw, it was difficult to imagine the detective ever returning to our screens without his boss and mentor telling him what to do.

Yet six years after Chief Inspector Morse dies of a heart attack, Lewis, now promoted to Detective Inspector Lewis, returns (in 2006) doing what he does best – solving murders in the academic world of Oxford – with his own sidekick, Detective Sergeant James Hathaway, played by Laurence Fox. His return, first in a pilot episode then a full series (and still going strong!), delighted fans, not just because writer Colin Dexter's tales are always so absorbing but because it gave them a chance to revisit all those Oxford haunts which helps make *Inspector Morse* so enjoyable to watch. Indeed, Oxford is a favoured town for many a location manager and has featured in the *Harry Potter* films, *Shadowlands*, *Midsomer Murders* and *Brideshead Revisited* to name but a few other productions.

Many Oxford colleges including Wadham in Parks Road, Trinity, Brasenose and Lincoln which featured as Lonsdale College in series two, Exeter and Hertford Colleges can be spotted in several episodes of *Lewis*, with often just the exteriors of these beautiful buildings used to double up for other venues. Corpus Christi College is used in episode one of series two and the crew were even allowed to film a scene on a roof that was under construction. In that same episode, filming also takes place at New College and University College where the Shelley Memorial is based.

"During the holidays most colleges are available for filming although two or three of them are unfortunately too expensive for television drama," said Nick Marshall who was Location Manager on series two of *Lewis*. "All the colleges we filmed at were very accommodating towards us. But on the other hand,

Above: **The beautiful Radcliffe Camera in Oxford.**

Sat nav references:

The Ashmolean Museum of Art and Archaeology (OX1 2PH)

Bodleian Library (OX1 3BG)

Botanic Garden (OX1 4AZ)

Corpus Christi College (OX1 4JF)

Hertford Colleges (OX1 3BW)

Lonsdale College (OX1 3DP)

Merton College (OX1 4JD)

New College (OX1 3BN)

Oriel College (OX1 4EW)

Turf Tavern (OX1 3SU)

University College (OX1 4BH)

nobody loses sight of the fact that the education of the students is the most important thing and we did find that once university holidays were over, we couldn't always film at certain colleges.

"Fortunately, Trinity allowed us to film for three and a half days during term time which was a great help." The well-kept grounds of virtually every Oxford college are ideal backdrops for Lewis and Hathaway, who are often seen strolling them while discussing their latest case.

Of course the distinguished, wood-panelled interiors of some of the colleges are also used in certain episodes. For instance, in *Old School Ties*, screened in 2007, the inside of Caroline's (Emma Campbell Webster) college room is shot at Merton College in Merton Street, while the porter's lodge of her college is filmed at Oriel College in Oriel Street.

The Principal's house of Hertford College also doubles up as the home of a character in episode four of series two. Nick was particularly delighted to receive permission to film at Oxford's renowned Bodleian Library in Broad Street which is the main library of the University of Oxford and is open to the public. In fact the library's Divinity Room and Exhibition room attract over 200,000 visitors a year.

"We did quite a lot at The Bodleian Library," said Nick, "particularly, and uniquely, in the basement and amongst the basement stacks, where a great many old and precious books are kept." For further information on the library, go to www.bodley.ox.ac.uk During the very early days of *Morse*, the production would be based in the centre of the city by the Radcliffe Camera until permission was withdrawn. This is exactly where *Lewis* was based during filming of the pilot and first series, much to the delight of the production team.

For series two, the unit base was situated at the car park of Oxpens Coach Park by the ice rink while Radcliffe Square was used to park essential equipment vehicles nearer to the centre of Oxford.

"The Police and the Council were most welcoming when I told them we were planning to return for another series, and were extremely helpful throughout," said Nick. There is of course more to Oxford than simply its seats of academia with the town centre itself, restaurants, hotels and stunning Botanic Garden in Rose Lane also featuring in *Lewis*. The Garden was established in 1621 making it the oldest botanic garden in the UK and the third oldest in the world. With thousands of species of plants, a magnificent greenhouse and walled section, it is a popular tourist attraction and well worth a visit. Telephone 01865 286690 to find out about opening times.

Fans of the show will recall seeing the Bridge of Sighs in more than one episode. This is to be found in New College Lane and its official name is Hertford Bridge. The reason it is commonly referred to as the Bridge of Sighs is because of its strong resemblance to the bridge of the same name in Venice. It was designed by Sir Thomas Jackson, finished in 1914 and links the old and new quadrangles of Hertford College.

If you're planning a visit to the city, why not stop for a drink at the Turf Tavern tucked away in Bath Place which with foundations linking back to the 14th Century, makes it the oldest pub in Oxford. Lewis and Hathaway can be seen enjoying a drink there in one episode, although the pair don't have a regular social haunt. If you do pop in, look out for the sketch of Inspector Morse on the wall. The Ashmolean Museum of Art and Archaeology features in *Lewis* on more than one occasion. Situated in Beaumont Street, it was founded in 1683 and is one of the oldest public museums in the world, offering a variety of exhibitions throughout the year and better still, no entry fee. Go to www. ashmolean.org for further information.

To the north west of Oxford is an area called Jericho consisting of rows and rows of terrace houses. Locals may recognise the area when they tune into repeats of *Lewis*, in particular Nelson Street where a large explosion was staged for one episode. Of course, not all scenes in *Lewis* are filmed in Oxford at all. For instance, West Car Park at Slough Railway Station doubled up as Oxford Railway Station in at least one scene while The Duke of Kent, Scotch Common in Ealing doubled up as an Oxford restaurant in an episode where Lewis has dinner with Diane Turnbull, played by Gina McKee. The old DHSS office in Ealing has been used for various interiors and Lewis' own flat is actually filmed in a property in Ealing while Hathaway's flat is in Shepherds Bush, West London.

Middlemarch

Stamford

Above (left): **Rufus Sewell as Will Ladislaw in *Middlemarch* and** (right) **Stamford, the main location for the 1994 BBC adaptation.**

Producers of the 1994 BBC serial *Middlemarch*, which starred Rufus Sewell as Will Ladislaw, Douglas Hodge as Tertius Lydgate and Juliet Aubrey as Dorothea Brooke, quite expected to have to film in many different towns in order to authentically recreate Victorian England. That was because virtually nowhere exists unaltered since the 1830s as Producer Louis Marks explained: "We presumed we'd have to film all over the country - a street here, a square there, a house somewhere else.

"But then our researchers came back and told us they'd found this marvellous town that had everything. So I went up to Lincolnshire, took one look and I knew they were right. Stamford is beautiful."

The town needed some ageing so period-style doors were placed over new ones and Georgian-type windows were hung over the top of modern ones. Locations used in the town included unspoiled St George's Square, Browne's Hospital and the area Barn Hill - which includes Number Three All Saints Place, which played Doctor Lydgate's home.

Outside the town centre Grimsthorpe Castle doubled as Qualingham. The castle, which was also used for scenes in *Moll Flanders* and *The Buccaneers*, is open to the public for much of the year. See www.grimsthorpe.co.uk for details.

The opening episode carriage scenes were filmed in Burghley Park. The Park is open all year and 16th Century Elizabethan Burghley House is open for much of the year. See www.burghley.co.uk for details.

Rambling Mill Lane and Stamford Arts Centre, which doubled as the White Hart Hotel, also appeared. In fact the Arts Centre, which also contains Stamford

Sat nav references:

Browne's Hospital (PE9 1PF)

Burghley Park (PE9 3JY)

Grimsthorpe Castle (PE10 0LY)

Number Three All Saints Place (PE9 2AG)

Stamford Arts Centre (PE9 2DL)

Tourist Information Centre, looked so much like a hotel after the BBC film team decorated it that several visitors to the town during filming tried to book rooms!

In 2004 the building, along with St George's Square and St Mary's Street, appeared in the film version of *Pride and Prejudice*, which stars Keira Knightley and Matthew Macfadyen. This time the town played the village of Meryton, home to the Bennet family.

Peak Practice

Crich

Above (top): **Wingfield Manor.** *(below)* **Dr Jack Kerruish (Kevin Whately) saves a life in a typical *Peak Practice* scene.**

Peak Practice became one of ITV's most successful drama series of the 90s. It began in 1993 starring Kevin Whately as Dr Jack Kerruish, Amanda Burton as Dr Beth Glover and Simon Shepherd as Dr Will Preston as the GPs at The Beeches surgery in the fictional village of Cardale. Over the years characters changed but it continued to be successful and ran until 2002.

The pretty Derbyshire village of Crich played Cardale and fans of the show can easily find plenty of locations. Even before you reach Crich marketplace you'll spot on your left, down the hill next to the Black Swan pub Archway House that played Dr Beth Glover's home.

Next you'll see the Costcutter shop which doubled as the bank in the series and a few doors along from that is the local fish and chip shop which was renamed The Cardale Fish and Chip Restaurant in honour of the series. The series' cast and crew often visited the shop while filming and Kevin Whately used to be a regular.

To find the house that played Dr Kerruish's home take a left turn down Dimple lane, go down for about a quarter of a mile until you see fields on your left, carry on further and you'll find private Melkridge House that played his home. Down the road in Bobbin Mill Hill, Fritchley is Chestnut Bank House, a large private house which played The Beeches surgery in the series.

The pub where Jack Kerruish got involved in a fight in an early episode of *Peak Practice* was actually The Manor Hotel, in nearby South Wingfield. Nearby Wingfield Manor, a ruined mansion now owned by English Heritage was used for Cardale's mediaeval pageant. For further details about the house, which was also used for Franco Zeffirelli's 1996 film *Jane Eyre* see www.englishheritage.org.uk

The church where Dr Erica Matthews jilted Dr Andrew Attwood during the 1998 series was St Peter's Church at Edensor inside Chatsworth Park. Dr David Shearer was hit and killed by a motorcycle at Elton and the funeral was filmed at St Giles Church at Hartington. Outside Crich locations all round the Peak District and in the magnificent Peak District National Park were regularly used.

Sat nav references:

Black Swan pub (DE4 5DD)

Cardale Fish and Chip Restaurant (DE4 5DD)

Chestnut Bank House (DE56 2HN)

Costcutter shop (DE4 5DD)

Melkridge House (DE56 2HP)

Upstairs, Downstairs

Leamington Spa

The original series of this popular costume drama was broadcast on London Weekend Television then BBC1 between 1971 and 1975 and much to the surprise of some executives, gradually became unmissable television.

Below: **London's fashionable 165 Eaton Place is actually an address in Leamington Spa, in** *Upstairs, Downstairs* (bottom) **Ellie Kendrick as maid Ivy Morris.**

A portrayal of upstairs aristocrats, the Bellamy family, and their downstairs servants, most of the drama takes place within the elegant walls of 165 Eaton Place, an address in the heart of fashionable London during the Edwardian era and beyond to 1930.

The house itself, a tall, impressive building with polished steps and gleaming front door, not to mention vast interior rooms and huge hallway, forms a significant part of the drama series and for a while, the address was instantly recognisable by millions of television fans who grew to love the surroundings as much as the characters. The exteriors are actually of 65 Eaton Place in London with the 1 painted in front, while the interiors are filmed at London Weekend Television's studios in Wembley then at The London Studios on the South Bank.

Fast forward to 2010 and *Upstairs, Downstairs* returned to BBC1 in December 2010, the story taking up six screen years after the last episode ended. The cast is different apart from actress and original creator Jean Marsh who reprises her role as Rose Buck and the residents are now Lord Holland, his wife Lady Agnes and their servants but the house in Eaton Place remains the same, albeit with a facelift. While Rose was a housemaid in the original series, she returns to Eaton Square as Housekeeper in the latest adaptation.

Once again, the hallway is a feature of the house and to diehard fans, the doorway couldn't belong anywhere other than to 165 Eaton Place. Anyone tuning in to *Upstairs, Downstairs* would be forgiven for believing the exterior scenes of the impressive property were shot in the heart of fashionable London as

Above (top): **Filming *Upstairs, Downstairs* in Leamington Spa and** *(Right)* **Claire Foy as Lady Persephone Towyn and Ellie Kendrick as Ivy Morris.**

they originally were. Remarkably they are actually filmed miles away at 42 Clarendon Square in Leamington Spa.

Location Manager Nicky May said the search for the perfect Eaton Place spread across London, Bath, Bristol, Cheltenham and initially, only London appeared to offer any possibilities, though filming there generally proves difficult. "We were looking in books and the director suddenly said he'd spotted a stucco-fronted house in Leamington," she revealed. "So it was just by chance that we found Clarendon Square. It's actually somebody's house and is split up into about eight flats inside; it's one of the biggest houses in the street. The first floor windows belong to the owner who has his office there.

"The owner was abroad at the time but I managed to get his permission to film the outside of his house and to use his hallway and front door. We only had to paint the hallway and that was it. As soon as you come into the front door you come on to the set and we put a false doorway beyond the front door. So there were very little changes to be made which made it all the more ideal for our purposes."

The stunning interiors of Eaton Place are created on specially constructed sets in South Wales and designed by Eve Stewart, Oscar-nominated designer on the award-winning film *The King's Speech*. The downstairs kitchen areas are built at Upper Boat Studios, Cardiff home of BBC1's *Doctor Who* while the main sitting room, the bedroom and the garage are filmed at Dragon Studio in Bridgend. The actual layout of the house is the same as in the earlier episodes with the staircase on the right hand side of the hall, all superbly designed by Eve.

Other locations of interest include the Ballroom at Claridges Hotel in London where the opening scenes of *Upstairs, Downstairs* are filmed and Mount Stuart Square in Cardiff, used to shoot political riot scenes. Cardiff University's Glamorgan Building doubles up as the Foreign Office, The Guildhall in Swansea becomes a railway station while the pub is especially built within the Coal Exchange in Cardiff.

Sat nav references:

Claridges Hotel (W1K 4HR)

Coal Exchange (CF10 5EB)

Glamorgan Building (CF10 3WA)

The Guildhall (SA1 4PE)

Leamington Spa (CV32 5QZ)

Vanity Fair

Warwickshire

Set during the Napoleonic Wars, William Makepeace Thackeray's classic novel *Vanity Fair* follows the life of Becky Sharp, the penniless, orphaned daughter of an artist and a French opera dancer and Amelia Sedley, the sheltered child of a rich city merchant. They make a pair of unlikely but firm friends who are very different in character. Becky is an irresistible schemer and will stop at nothing to get what she wants whereas Amelia is meek and mild.

The lavish 1998 BBC adaptation of *Vanity Fair* starred Natasha Little as Becky, Frances Grey as Amelia, Nathaniel Parker as red-blooded Rawdon Crawley and Tom Ward as dashing officer George Osborne.

Below: **Two views of stunning Stowe Landscape Gardens, used as Hyde Park, London in *Vanity Fair*.**

The series took 21 weeks to film and was shot in locations as diverse as London, Paris, the Rhine Valley and the coast of West Wales. The Ballroom scene was filmed at Cheltenham Town Hall and the town's Pittville Pump Room was used as a foreign restaurant for another scene. Both are open to the public and part of the Pump Room is now a museum.

The beach and several rows of houses in Tenby, Wales doubled as Brighton and Ragley Hall, Warwickshire, played the home of Lord Steyne. Claydon House at Middle Claydon, Buckinghamshire played the interior of a hotel in Germany. It is owned by the National Trust and is open to the public as are Stowe Landscape Gardens at Buckingham, Buckinghamshire, a stunning survivor of Georgian times which doubled as Hyde Park.
See www.nationaltrust.org.uk

Sat nav references:

Cheltenham Town Hall (GL50 1QA)

Claydon House (MK18 2EY)

Stowe Landscape Gardens (MK18 5DQ)

Wales

Casualty
Doctor Who
Classic Doctor Who
Gavin and Stacey
The Prisoner
Sherlock

Casualty

Cardiff

When *Casualty* was launched in 1986, no one could have predicted it would become television's longest-running medical drama, pulling in millions of viewers and winning several awards including a BAFTA for the best continuing drama in 2007. Set in Holby City Hospital in the fictional city of Holby, the series was filmed in Bristol until 2011. Over the years many city landmarks could be seen. For instance, the Clifton Suspension Bridge and the floating harbour have made quite a few appearances.

Until 2011 most of *Casualty* was shot at a specially-constructed set inside an industrial warehouse in the St Phillips area of Bristol as it was decided early on, after the BBC's production team visited almost every hospital in Bristol, that trying to film a television series within a real-life working hospital simply wouldn't work.

For 16 years *Casualty* exterior shots were filmed at the Brunel College of Arts and Technology (now the Ashley Down Centre), part of City of Bristol College. In 2002, a new exterior set was built at St Phillips, close to the interior set, so that virtually all filming could be done in one location. In 2011 the BBC decided to shift filming to Cardiff where a purpose built set was constructed.

Doctor Who

Cardiff

Above and opposite (top): **Christopher Eccleston and Billie Piper filming scenes for *The Unquiet Dead* in Swansea.**

Since its return in 2005 *Doctor Who* has been a huge success for the BBC - and a fantastic boost for the city of Cardiff where the show is produced. The production team has been very inventive and locations all over the city and in the wider area have been used to play both places on earth and further afield. The following list provides details of many of the key places used for filming.

The Ninth Doctor - Christopher Eccleston

Series One (2005)
Rose
Howells department store (Henrik's department store), University Hospital of Wales (Henrik's basement), La Fosse restaurant (Tizano's restaurant), Cardiff Royal Infirmary (restaurant yard), Queen's Arcade, Working Street (shopping centre), disued Ely Papermill, Grangetown (Nestene's lair), Flats at Lydstep Crescent, Gabalfa (all Cardiff), Royal Air Force memorial, Embankment, London

The End of The World
Temple of Peace Hall (reception area), BBC Broadcasting House, Churchill Way (corridors) both in Cardiff

The Unquiet Dead
White Swan Court (NP25 3NY) (Tardis lands), Beaufort Arms Court, Monmouth (outside of Sneed's undertakers), New Theatre, Cardiff (theatre), The Exchange Building, Swansea (theatre exterior), Headlands School, Penarth (chapel of rest), Cambrian Place, Swansea (street)

Aliens of London
Cardiff Royal Infirmary (Albion Hospital), Hensol Castle, Vale of Glamorgan (inside Downing Street), John Adam Street, London (Downing Street), Westminster Bridge and Tower Bridge, London (themselves)

World War III
John Adam Street, London (Downing Street), Brandon Estate, Kennington, London (Tardis crashes), Lower Dock Street, Newport (the remains of Downing Street), Hensol Castle, Vale of Glamorgan (inside Downing Street)

Dalek
Corridors and staircase under Millennium Stadium, Cardiff (CF10 1JA)

The Long Game
Filmed in a studio

Father's Day
Office at ITV Wales (register office), St Paul's Church, Grangetown (church), Loudoun Square, Butetown, Cardiff (Pete is run over), Paget Street, Grangetown (street), St Fagan's Street, Cardiff (Tardis lands)

The Empty Child
Headlands School, Penarth (nightclub), Cardiff Royal Infirmary (Albion Hospital), Barry Island railway www.valeofglamorganrailway.co.uk (railway station), Womanby Street (street)

The Doctor Dances
See *The Empty Child*

Boom Town
Roald Dahl Plass, Cardiff Bay (Tardis lands), Glamorgan Building, Cardiff University (city hall), The Bosphorus, Cardiff Bay (restaurant). Other scenes filmed at Mermaid Quay and Cardiff Central station

Bad Wolf
Flat at Severn Square, Cardiff (Big Brother House)

The Parting of the Ways
Loudoun Square, Butetown, Cardiff (the Tyler's estate), Paddle Steamer Cafe, Loudoun Square (chip shop), playground at Canal Park, Butetown

Above: **Billie Piper** as seen in *The Idiot's Lantern.*

The Tenth Doctor - David Tennant

The Christmas Invasion
Howells department store (Henrik's department store), Millennium Stadium loading areas (UNIT HQ). Baltic House in Mount Stuart Square, Cardiff (fire escape), British Gas Building, Tredegar House, Newport (Downing Street interior), Clearwell Caves, Gloucestershire www.clearwellcaves.com (Sycorax spaceship interior), Barry Docks (Sycorax spaceship), Tower of London (UNIT HQ exterior)

Series Two (2006)
New Earth
Worm's Head at Rhossili - Gower Peninsula (Rose and the Doctor admire New Earth), Wales Millennium Centre, Cardiff Bay (alien Hospital), Tredegar House, Newport (basement), disused Ely Papermill, Cardiff (testing lab), Ba Orient, Cardiff Bay (nightclub)

Tooth and Claw
Gelligaer Common, Fochriiw, Merthyr (Tardis lands), Craig-Y-Nos Castle, Brecon Beacons - www.craigynoscastle.com (Sir Robert's House), Penllyn Castle, Cowbridge (courtyard), Headlands School, Penarth (corridor), Tredegar House, Newport (various interiors)

School Reunion
Belle View Park (Tardis lands), Duffryn High School, Newport (school), Fitzalan High School, Canton, Cardiff (school), Da Vinci's Coffee Shop, High Street, Newport (coffee shop), Belle Vue Park, Newport (Doctor says farewell to Sarah Jane)

The Girl in the Fireplace
Dyffryn Gardens, Vale of Glamorgan - www.dyffryngardens.org.uk (Palace of Versailles), Ragley Hall, Alcester - www.ragleyhall.com (Versailles ballroom)

Rise of the Cybermen
Riverfront Arts Centre, Newport (Tardis arrives), South Side Roath Dock, Cardiff Docks (recruitment area), Cardiff Heliport (President's arrival), Mount Stuart Square, Cardiff Bay (street), Sanatorium Road, Cardiff (army checkpoint), Compton Street, Grangetown (Mickey snatched), Coedarhydyglyn House, near Cardiff– private residence (the Tyler home), Lambeth Pier, Albert Embankment, London (Tardis arrives)

The Age of Steel
Newport Docks (Cybermen give chase), Grangemoor Park (making plans scene), Magor Brewery, Bridgend (humans converted), Uskmouth Power Station (Cyberfactory)

The Idiot's Lantern
Shop in Blenheim Road, Cardiff (Magpie Electricals), Florentia Street (Florizel Street), South Dock, Newport Docks (Bishop's HQ), Cardiff Royal Infirmary (Alexandra Palace), Cardiff Heliport (top of transmitter)

The Impossible Planet
Mamhilad Park Industrial Estate, Pontypool (Ood holding pens), Wenvoe Quarry, Cardiff (planet surface)

The Satan Pit
Clearwell Caves in Gloucestershire (The Satan Pit)

Love & Monsters
Cargo Road, Cardiff Docks (Woolwich), Impounding station, Newport Docks (Elton tries to find the Doctor), Heol Pentwyn, Cardiff (Elton's home), The Hayes, Cardiff (London shopping street). Llandaff Fields, Cardiff (Elton meets Ursula), Jacob's Antiques, West Canal Wharf (LI'n'DA headquarters), St David's Market, Cardiff (looking for Jackie), Adam Street Car Park (The Doctor meets the Abzorbaloff), St. Peter's Sport and Social Club, Minster Road, Cardiff (Elton and his mother)

Fear Her
Page Drive, Cardiff (Kelly Holmes Close), Storage Yard, Newport Road, Cardiff (East London), Millennium Stadium (Olympic Stadium) in Cardiff, St Alban's Rugby Club (Doctor light's torch)

Army of Ghosts
St Mary Street (Rose on bus), Southerndown beach, Ogmore Vale, Vale of Glamorgan (alien world), Brandon Estate, Kennington, London (Powell Estate), Loudoun Square, Cardiff (Tyler estate), aircraft hanger RAF St Athlan (Torchwood), Brackla Bunkers, Bridgend (Torchwood corridors), Broadstairs Road, Cardiff (Cybermen attack house), One Canada Square, London (Torchwood Tower), Compass Bridge Road, Cardiff Docks (battle)

Doomsday
See *Army of Ghosts*, plus: Broadstairs Road, Cardiff (Cybermen march), Coedarhydyglyn House, near Cardiff – private residence (the Tyler home), Southerndown beach, Ogmore Vale, Vale of Glamorgan (Doctor and Rose say goodbye)

Above: **The Doctor (David Tennant) in fine voice and** *(below)* **Billie Piper makes a surprise appearance in** ***Partners In Crime.***

Left: **The Doctor (David Tennant) and Rose (Billie Piper).**

Above: **The Doctor (David Tennant) and Donna (Catherine Tate) in a scene from *The Runaway Bride*.**

The Runaway Bride

St John the Baptist at Trinity Street, Cardiff (St Mary's Church, Chiswick), Churchill Way, Cardiff (Tardis lands), Old Library, The Hayes, Cardiff (evil santas), Wall next to Waterstones, Wharton Street, Cardiff (cashpoint), A4232 at Leckwith and Great West Road, Chiswick (Tardis chase), Atradius, Cardiff Bay (Donna's workplace), Baverstock Hotel, Merthyr Tydfil (evil santas invade wedding reception - interior), New Country House Hotel, Thornhill, Cardiff (wedding reception – exterior), Millennium Stadium (Tardis lands underground), Impound station, Newport Docks (the empress's lair), St Mary Street, Cardiff (tank), International Press Centre, Shoe Lane, London (rooftop), Princes Avenue, Cardiff (Donna's parents' home)

Series Three (2007)

Smith & Jones

University of Glamorgan (Royal Hope Hospital interior) and Singleton Hospital, Swansea (exterior), Outside Blueberry Hotel and Grill, Market Street, Pontypridd (Jones family row), Queen Street, Cardiff (outside the Royal Hope), Quay Street, Cardiff (Martha on the phone)

The Shakespeare Code

Ford's Hospital, Greyfriar's Lane, Coventry (London streets), Cheylesmore Manor House, Coventry (street) Lord Leycester Hospital, Warwick - www.lordleycester.com (street), Shakespeare's Globe, London (The Globe Theatre), Blueberry Hotel and Grill, Pontypridd (Shakespeare's room), Newport Indoor Market (Bedlam)

Gridlock

Temple of Peace, Cardiff (New York Senate building), Ely Papermill, Cardiff (warehouses), The Maltings, Cardiff Bay (alley)

Daleks in Manhattan
Cogan playing fields, Penarth (Tardis lands), Park and Dare Theatre, Treorchy (theatre), Trident Park, Cardiff Bay (Dalek Base), Bute Park, Cardiff (Central Park), Headlands School, Penarth (theatre backstage)

Evolution of the Daleks
See Daleks in Manhattan, plus: Treberfydd House, Llangasty, Brecon www.treberfydd.com (Hooverville Guard)

The Lazarus Experiment
Wells Cathedral, Wells (Southwark Cathedral), Senedd Building, Welsh Assembly, Cardiff, (Lazarus Institute), Sir William House, Tresillian Terrace, Cardiff (Lazarus's office), National Museum of Wales, Cardiff (press conference), Biomedical Science Building, Cardiff University (laboratory)

42
House in Cwrt-y-Vil Road, Penarth (Francine's House), Trident Park, Cardiff Bay (ship control panels), St Regis Paper Company mill, Caldicot (space ship)

Human Nature
Treberfydd House, Llangasty, Brecon - www.treberfydd.com (Farringham School), Llandaf Cathedral, Cardiff (school dormitory and war memorial), Tredegar House, Newport (school), St Fagan's National Museum, Cardiff (village and dance hall)

The Family of Blood
See Human Nature, plus: Neal Soil Supplies, Rumney, Cardiff (First World War battlefield)

Blink
Former NatWest Bank, Bute Street, Cardiff (police station), West Bute Street, Cardiff (outside the pub), Miners Hospital, Caerphilly (Welgrove Hospice), St Woolos Cemetery, Newport (Kathy's Grave), House at 18 Fields Park Avenue, Newport (Wester Drumlins), Alexandra Gardens, Cathays Park, Cardiff (site of statues), Chartist Tower, Newport (Billy meets the Doctor and Martha)

Utopia
Trident Park, Cardiff Bay (radiation room and corridors), Roald Dahl Plass, Cardiff (rift site), Argoed Quarry, Llanharry (surface of Malcassairo), Wenvoe Quarry, Wenvoe (rocket silo site)

The Sound of Drums
Fortes, Paget Road, Barry Island (café), Hensol Castle (Downing Street), Cwrt-y-Vil Road, Penarth (Francine's and Clive's homes), Maelfa Shopping Centre, Llanedeyrn, Cardiff (The Doctor and the Master talk), Wenallt Road, Caerphilly (hillside), RAF St Athan (airstrip), Whitmore Bay, Barry Island (timelord initiation), Penarth Esplanade (Martha warns Leo), University Place, Cardiff (outside Martha's flat). Other locations: The Friary, Cardiff, High Street, Penarth, Millennium Square, Cardiff

Above: **Freema Agyeman as Martha Jones** *Below:* **Catherine Tate as Donna Noble in *Partners in Crime*.**

Above: **The return of the Cyberman**

Last of the Time Lords
See *The Sound of Drums*, plus: Vaynor Quarry, Merthyr Tydfil (the Doctor confronts the Master), Whitmore Bay, Barry Island (Martha arrives), Roald Dahl Plass, Cardiff (farewell to Jack), Alexandra Gardens, Cardiff (Martha gives flowers). Also used: Aberthaw Power Station, Barry

Voyage of the Damned
Mamhilad Industrial Estate (Deck 31), The Coal Exchange, Cardiff Bay (Titanic lounge), Working Street, Cardiff (passengers teleport and London street), inside Exchange Building, Cambrian Place, Swansea (Titanic teleport)

Partners in Crime
Helmont House, Churchill Way, Cardiff (Adispose Industries), Odeon Cinema, Cardiff (presentation), Toilets at Tiger, Tiger, Cardiff (toilets), Fat Cat Café, Greyfriars, Cardiff (café), Nant-Fawr Road, Cardiff (Donna's home), Charles Street, Cardiff

The Fires of Pompeii
Cinecittà Film Studios, Rome (private), Temple of Peace, Cardiff (Temple), Clearwell Caves, Gloucestershire (inside the volcano), Morlais Quarry, Merthyr Tydfil (Mount Vesuvius slopes)

Planet of the Ood
Lafarge Cement, Barry (Ood compound), Trefil Quarry, Tredegar (Ood Sphere), Mamhilad Park Industrial Estate, Pontypool (warehouse)

The Sontaran Stratagem
Margam Country Park, Port Talbot (academy), Compass Bridge Road, Cardiff (car goes into water), Cargo Road (Atmos controls jeep), Mamhilad Park Industrial Estate, Pontypool (factory)

The Poison Sky
See *The Sontaran Stratagem*

The Doctor's Daughter
Newbridge Memo, Newbridge (human base), Plantasia Botanic Gardens, Swansea (the Source), Kenfig Hill, Bridgend (Messaline), Barry Shooting Range (bunker)

The Unicorn and the Wasp
Cefn Llwyd lake, Caerphilly (lake), St Senwyr's Church, Cowbridge (church), Hensol Castle - www.hensol.co.uk (The Harrogate Hotel), Llansannor Court (Edison Manor)

Silence in the Library
42 Palace Road Cardiff (flat), Brangwyn Hall, Swansea (Library Entrance), Central Library, Swansea (Library)

The Forest of the Dead
Hansol Castle, Glamorgan (Donna and Lee's room/ The riverside), Victoria Park, Canton, Cardiff (Donna meets veiled woman), Crwys Medical Centre, Cardiff (Donna has twins), St Mary of the Angels, Kings Road, Cardiff (Donna's wedding), 42 Palace Road, Canton, Cardiff (Cal's house), 38 Palace Road,

Cardiff (Donna and Lee's house), Palace Road, Canton, Cardiff (veiled woman in street), Dyffryn Gardens, St. Nicholas, Vale of Glamorgan (The hospital), Dyffryn House, St. Nicholas, Vale of Glamorgan (The hospital/Donna's children's bedroom), Brangwyn Hall, Swansea (The library entrance/hall), Alcoa, Swansea (The library core), Central Library, Swansea (the library)

Midnight
Celtic Manor Forum Spa, Usk Valley, Newport (Pool side)

Turn Left
Bay Chambers, West Bute Street, Cardiff (Chowdry's Office), Hunter Street, Cardiff (The Doctor's body), Clearwater Way, Cardiff (Donna arrives back in time), Nant-Fawr Road, Cardiff (Donna and Sylvia drive to work), Court Road, Cardiff (Donna decides), Heol Gabriel, Cardiff (Donna drives past traffic jam), Lady Mary Allotments, Roath Park, Cardiff (Wilf sees the stars vanish), St Isan Road, Cardiff (Donna jumps in front of a lorry), Franklen Road, Cardiff (Donna meets Rose), The Maltings Ltd, Cardiff (Shan Shen Alley), Cardiff Royal Infirmary, Newport Road, Cardiff (Royal Hope Hospital), Blackton Lane, Porthkerry (Donna's family sent to Leeds), Egerton Grey Country House Hotel, Porthkerry (Donna and family check in), Porthkerry Viaduct, Porthkerry (Hotel guests watch London being destroyed), 7 Machen Street, Cardiff (Donna's family are placed in a home in Leeds), Rudry Street, Cardiff (Donna meets Rose), The Conway Pub, Cardiff (christmas party in pub), Mortimer Road, Cardiff (people watch the Christmas Star attack), Sophia Gardens, Cardiff (Donna talks to Rose in park), Avesta Polarit Panteg Steelworks, Newport (UNIT warehouse)

The Stolen Earth
Nant-Fawr Road (house interior), Cardiff (Rose listens to Harriet at Wilf's), Optometry and Visual Sciences, Cardiff University (the Shadow Proclamation), Ffordd Gerdinan, Tonteg, Mid Glamorgan (the Tardis lands on Earth), Outside 18 Hawthorn Road, Pontypridd (Wilf and Sylvia look up into sky) Market Street, Pontypridd (Rose watches the Dalek saucers attack), High Street, Penarth (the Tardis materialises on Earth), Queens Road, Penarth (Rose materialises), Paget Road, Penarth (a Dalek appears and shoots Doctor), Arcot Street, Penarth (Jack materialises and destroys Dalek), Brook Street, Cardiff (Daleks round up humans), Plantagenet Street, Cardiff (a Dalek confronts Wilf and Silvia), South Wales Traffic Management Centre, Coryton, Cardiff (UNIT HQ in New York), Lower House, Michaelston-le-Pit (Harriet's house), Wales Museum Collections Centre, Barry Island (Martha taken to Project Idigo), Cwrt-y-Vil Road, Penarth (Martha materialises at mother's), 21 Clinton Road, Penarth (Sarah drives to meet the Doctor), Robinswood Crescent, Penarth (Sarah's car stopped by Dalek patrol), Roald Dahl Plass, Cardiff (the Torchwood Hub signals the Doctor)

Journey's End
Nant-Fawr Road, Cardiff (outside Wilf's), Southerndown Beach, Ogmore Vale, Bridgend (the Doctor drops off Rose and new family back at Bad Wolf Bay), Hawthorn Road, Pontypridd (Wilf and Sylvia watch Dalek ships leave), High Street, Penarth (Tardis transferred to the Crucible), Arcot Street, Penarth (Sarah-Jane, Mickey and Jackie surrender to Daleks), Castell Coch, Cardiff (UNIT Germany), Mir Street (formerly Alpha Street), Newport (inside the Crucible), Morgan Jones Park, Caerphilly (the Doctor drops his friends back),

Above: **Kylie Minogue takes a break from filming *Voyage of the Damned* in Swansea.**

Cwrt-y-Vil Road, Penarth (Martha says goodbye to Francine), Robinswood Crescent, Penarth (Sarah's car stopped by Daleks)

The Next Doctor (2008 Christmas Special)

Fonmon Castle, Rhoose, Vale of Glamorgan (inside Reverend Fairchild's house), St Woolos Cemetery, Newport (the funeral), The Maltings Ltd, Cardiff (the Doctor meets The Doctor), MOD Caerwent, Monmouthshire (Inside the warehouse), Tredegar House, Newport (the Doctor's base, and Tardis courtyard), Hensol Castle, Glamorgan (cellar/tunnels), Millers Green, Gloucester (the Doctor arrives in Victorian London), College Green, Gloucester (the funeral procession), Berkeley Street, Gloucester (Jackson shelters with a child), Shire Hall, Monmouth (outside the Cyberbase)

Planet of the Dead

Gorsedd Gardens Road, Cardiff (outside Gallery), National Museum of Wales, Cardiff (gallery), A4232 (Grangetown/Butetown link), East Tunnel, Cardiff (the tunnel), The Friary (alley), Cardiff (Christina runs), Lloyd George Avenue, Cardiff Bay (chatting on the bus), St Mary's Street, Cardiff (Christina and Doctor board the bus), Mir Steel (formerly Alpha Steel), Newport (inside the Tritovore spaceship), Dubai Desert, UAE (the Planet of the Dead)

The Waters of Mars

Cemex (Taffs Well), Pentyrch, Cardiff (surface of Mars), National Botanic Garden of Wales, Carmarthenshire (Hydroponics Centre), Victoria Place, Newport (Adelaide's home), Next Generation Data (formerly Hynix Semiconductors), Imperial Park, Newport (base infrastructure/tunnels), Brandon Estate, Kennington, London (Tardis)

Below: **You thought the Tardis just appears... two members of the** *Doctor Who* **team assemble the famous blue box on location.**

The End of Time

Blackwells Bookshop, Cardiff University (book-signing), Tredegar House, Newport (Naismith residence), Corus Strip Products UK, Newport, Nant-Fawr Road, Cardiff (Donna's house), 11 Nant-Fawr Road, Cardiff (Donna's house), St. Mary's Church, Marshfield, Newport (Donna gets married), Clinton Road, Penarth (Donna meets Master), Victoria Road, Penarth (Doctor saves Luke), Portland Street, Swansea (Wilf and Doctor outside cafe), Kardomah Cafe, Swansea (Wilf and the Doctor discuss Donna), The Port of Cardiff, Cardiff Docks, Wales (the Doctor chases the Master), Mir Steel, Newport (warehouses), Cemex (Taffs Well), Pentyrch, Cardiff (The Oodsphere surface), Wookey Hole Caves, Wells, Somerset (the Council of the Ood's chamber), South Wales Traffic Management Centre, Coryton, Cardiff, Wharton Street, Cardiff (Wilf makes his way through the Christmas throng), Paget Road, Penarth (Doctor finds prison), St Augustines Church, Penarth (Wilf meets the mysterious woman), Caerphilly castle, Caerphilly (master resurrected), City Hall, Cardiff (The White House), Tiger Tiger, The Friary, Cardiff, Jesson House, Southwark, London (Humans become The Master), Brandon Estate, Kennington, London, River Severn, Gloucestershire (aerial shots)

The Eleventh Doctor - Matt Smith

Series Five
The Eleventh Hour
St Cadoc's hospital, Caerleon, Gwent (hospital exterior/Entrance/Locker Room), A48 (near Imperial Park), Newport (the Doctor drives to the hospital),

A48 (Castleton), Newport (the Doctor drives to the hospital), Mamhilad Park Industrial Estate (Dupont Factory), Pontypool, Wales (the roof of the hospital), The White House, Llandaff, Cardiff (Mrs Angelo's downstairs), The Cathedral Green, Llandaff, Cardiff (Leadworth), The Vicarage, Rhymney, Gwent (Amy's home), Abertillery Hospital, Aberbeeg, Abertillery (hospital corridors/wards), Llandaff Cathedral (lane), Llandaff, Cardiff (the Doctor and Amy walk into Leadworth)

The Beast Below
West Cross AAOR, Swansea (Churchill's Office), Neath Abbey, Swansea (beneath the Tower), Mamhilad Park Industrial Estate, Pontypool, Wales (within starship), Margam Country Park (orangery), Swansea (Liz's bedroom)

Victory of The Daleks
West Cross AAOR, Swansea (map room/Churchill's office), Glamorgan Building (rooftop), Cardiff University, Cardiff (rooftop), Jacob's Antique Centre, West Canal Wharf, Cardiff (Bracewell's laboratory), Brackla Bunkers, Bridgend (corridor/storage area), JR Freeman Cigars, Cardiff (Dalek ship)

The Time of Angels
Southerndown Beach, Ogmore Vale, Bridgend (the Tardis lands on Alfava Metraxis), Aberthaw Quarry, Fonmon, South Glamorgan (outside Temple), Clearwell Caves – Ancient Iron Mines, Coleford Gloucestershire (maze of the dead), Bute Park, Cardiff (security guard hallucinates), Brecon Cathedral, Brecon (the museum), The Vicarage, Rhymney, Gwent (Doctor bites Amy's hand)

Above: **The Doctor (Matt Smith) uses his sonic screwdriver** *Below:* **Karen Gillan in one of her first episodes as Amy Pond.**

Flesh and Stone
Southerndown Beach, Ogmore Vale, Bridgend (River says goodbye), Puzzlewood, Coleford, Gloucestershire (the Forest), Clearwell Caves – Ancient Iron Mines, Coleford, Gloucestershire (maze of the dead), The Vicarage, Rhymney, Gwent (Amy's home)

The Vampires of Venice
Bowls Inn, Newport (Rory's stag night), Trogir, Croatia, Pantana, Croatia, Atlantic College, St. Donat's, Llancaiach Fawr Manor, Nelson (Isabella's fathers kitchen), Caerphilly Castle, Caerphilly (the tunnels of Calvierri Mansion), Castell Coch, Cardiff

Amy's Choice
Skenfrith, Monmouthshire (Upper Leadworth), Sarn, Monmouthshire (Upper Leadworth), Skenfrith Castle, Monmouthshire (the castle ruins), House (off St Athan Road), Llanfair (Amy and Rory's home), College Street, Llantwit Major (Doctor staggers down a street), Church Street, Llantwit Major (Doctor staggers to a shop), Alan Young Butcher's, Church Street, Llantwit Major (inside butcher's), Eglwysilan Road (Church of St Ilan), Eglwysilan, Caerphilly (the Doctor drops off villagers), Lanelay Hall, Pontyclun (inside OAP home)

The Hungry Earth
St. Gwynno's Church, Llanwonno (the Church), Bedwellty Pits, Tredegar, Blaenau Gwent (pit housing), Tower Colliery, Hirwaun (the pit works)

Above (top): **Karen Gillan rests between scenes** *(above)*
Filming *Doctor Who* **on location on Southerndown Beach near Bridgend.**

Cold Blood

Bute Park, Cardiff (Amy remembers time with Rory), St. Gwynno's Church, Llanwonno (the Church), Tower Colliery, Hirwaun (drill site), Temple of Peace, Cardiff (Silurian Senate Chamber), Plantasia Botanic Gardens, Swansea (the Doctor and Nasreen are taken through city)

Vincent and The Doctor

Llandaff Cathedral, Cardiff (church), National Museum of Wales, Cardiff (Musee d'Orsay), Trogir, Croatia (the village centre), Vrsine, Croatia (fields around the village), Neath Abbey, Swansea (battling the monster Roald Dahl Plass), Cardiff (Tardis lands outside Musee d'Orsay)

The Lodger

Westville Road, Cardiff (outside Craig's house), Mill Gardens, Cardiff (the Tardis tries to materialise), Victoria Park, Canton, Cardiff (the Doctor is stranded), Lanelay Hall, Pontyclun (Craig's office)

The Pandorica Opens

Vrsine, Croatia (Vincent's home), Millennium Stadium, Cardiff (Stormcage facility), Brackla Bunkers, Bridgend (Churchill and Bracewell discuss the painting), Crystal, Cardiff (River barters for a vortex manipulator), The Vicarage, Rhymney, Gwent (River visits Amy's house), Stonehenge, Wiltshire (Stonehenge), Margam Country Park, Port Talbot (Roman Camp/Stonehenge), Gelligaer Common, Fochriiw, Merthyr (the Doctor, Amy and River race to Stonehenge)

The Big Bang

Puzzlewood, Coleford, Gloucestershire (Doctor tells Amy to remember), Brangwyn Hall, Swansea (inside museum), Gorsedd Gardens Road, Cardiff (Amy and aunt visit the museum), National Museum of Wales, Cardiff (Inside museum), Miskin Manor, Miskin (the wedding reception), The Vicarage, Rhymney, Gwent (back at Amy's house), Margam Country Park, Port Talbot (Stonehenge), Westville Road, Cardiff (The Doctor sees Amy noting the address)

Series Six

A Christmas Carol (2010 Christmas Special)

The Coal Exchange, Mount Stuart Square, Cardiff Bay, Mamhilad Park Industrial Estate, Pontypool, Wales (Kazran's study), Mir Steel, Newport (the township)

The Impossible Astronaut

Tredegar House, Newport (The Doctor is found beneath the skirt) Le Monde, Cardiff (Canton is picked up at bar), Glamorgan Building, Cardiff University (White House corridors), Eddie's Diner, Cardiff (the Doctor Catches

up with River), Millennium Stadium, Cardiff (The Stormcage Facility), I163 (Monument Valley), Utah (Amy, Rory, the Doctor and River meet up), Lone Rock Beach, Utah (The Doctor has a picnic by the lake)

Day of the Moon
Le Monde, Cardiff (People watch the Apollo landing), West Bute Street, Cardiff (River falls), Millennium Stadium, Cardiff (The Stormage facility), The Coal Exchange, Mount Stuart Square, Cardiff Bay (Offices), Troy House, Monmouthshire (The childrens home), MOD St Athan, Vale of Glamorgan (The Doctor is locked up in Area 51), Crockherbtown Lane, Cardiff (New York), I163 Monument Valley, Utah (Amy is shot), Glen Canyon Dam, Page, Arizona (Rory is shot)

The Curse of The Black Spot
Aboard The Phoenix, Charlestown, Cornwall (The Fancy)

The Doctor's Wife
Cemex, Pentyrch, Cardiff (House)

The Rebel Flesh
Cardiff Castle, Cardiff (the Monastery), Caerphilly Castle, Caerphilly (the Monastery shoreline, chambers), Neath Abbey, Swansea (the Monastery (Chapel), Atlantic College, St. Donat's (the Monastery), Chepstow Castle, Monmouthshire (The Monastery)

The Almost People
Cardiff Castle, Cardiff (the Monastery), Caerphilly Castle, Caerphilly (the Monastery), Neath Abbey, Swansea (the Monastery chapel), Atlantic College, St. Donat's (the Monastery), Senedd Building, Cardiff (the mainland base)

A Good Man Goes To War
Millennium Stadium, Cardiff (stormcage Facility), Laguna Health and Spa, The Friary, Cardiff (Dorium's Offices), Uskmouth Power Station, Newport (Demons Run), Lafarge Cement, Aberthaw (Battlefield (sontaran segement)), Fillcare Ltd, Talbot Green, Wales (cybership), MOD St Athan, Vale of Glamorgan (Demons Run main hall)

Above (top left): **Hugh Bonneville as Captain Henry Avery, Matt Smith and Karen Gillan film a scene about The Pheonix in Charlestown** *Above (top):* **Matt Smith and Karen Gillan on location on Southerndown Beach** *Below:* **The Doctor (Matt Smith).**

Classic Doctor Who

In the 45 years since *Doctor Who* began, the time travelling Doctor has been all over the galaxy - without leaving Earth! Credit must go to the show's many location managers who, over the years, have managed to find dozens of British locations to play either far-off planets or Earth in the past, present or future. What follows are some of the more interesting locations used over the years for filming of the classic series of *Doctor Who* - but clearly it is not an exhaustive list.

The First Doctor - William Hartnell (1963-1966)

Back in 1964, when the late William Hartnell played the Doctor, the dreaded Daleks invade the planet in the story *The Dalek Invasion of Earth* and are seen roaming in London near the Houses of Parliament, in Trafalgar Square, on Westminster Bridge, on the South Bank, at Whitehall, at the Albert Memorial. The footage shot in Trafalgar Square was shot at 5am and was supposed to show deserted London where everyone was hiding away from the Daleks. It looked deserted - except that if you look very carefully you will see a bus! The 1966 story *The Smugglers* was filmed at Nanjizal Bay in Cornwall.

Below: **Jon Pertwee on location in Portsmouth for the filming of *The Sea Devils*.**

The Second Doctor - Patrick Troughton (1966-1969)

Doctor number two, played by the late Patrick Troughton, lands his Tardis at Gatwick Airport in the story *The Faceless Ones*. The Nant Ffrancon Pass and Ogwen Lake in Snowdonia, Wales, played a more exotic location: Tibet, home of the Yeti - or so it appeared - in the 1967 story *The Abominable Snowman*. But when the Yeti takes over the London underground in *The Web of Fear*, London Transport demanded so high a fee for the use of its tube tunnels - and then only in the early hours of the morning - that the BBC filmed most of the story on studio sets. Climping Beach, Littlehampton, West Sussex was used for *The Enemy of the World*. The series took to the sea - well, the Thames Estuary - for the 1968 story *Fury From The Deep*, filming on the Radio 390 Offshore Platform at Red Sands and on the beach at Kingsgate in Kent. One of the series' most visually spectacular location sequences came in the 1968 story *The Invasion* when a supposedly massive army of Cybermen sweeps into London. After emerging from sewers, the Cybermen were later seen descending the steps with St Paul's Cathedral in the background. The quarries seen in *The Krotons* were in Malvern, Worcestershire and a string of locations in West Sussex including Clayton and East and West Dean were used for *The War Games*.

The Third Doctor - Jon Pertwee (1970-1974)

When the late Jon Pertwee took over the role of the Doctor in 1970 he came face to face in his first adventure with plastic monsters, the Autons, in *Spearhead from Space*. In another eerie sequence, the Autons, in the guise of tailors' dummies, came alive in a shop window, smashed their way out and started walking down the street shooting people. This scene was filmed early one Sunday morning in Ealing High Street in north London. The inside of Madame Tussauds in London was also used for a scene. The story also called for scenes at a hospital and at the headquarters of the United Nations Intelligence Task Force (UNIT) - and these were shot at the BBC's Engineering Training Centre at Wood Norton, near Evesham. In the 1971 story *The Mind of Evil*, Dover Castle played a prison where the evil Master, played by Roger

Delgado, is being kept under lock and key. During the story prisoners take over the prison and the authorities send in UNIT troops to storm it in one of the programme's finest action sequences. Later that year the Wiltshire village of Aldbourne played the fictional village of Devil's End in the popular story *The Daemons*. The village pub, The Blue Boar, doubled as The Cloven Hoof and the village church was used as the church. The barrow, which played Devil's Hump in the series, is about 1/4 of a mile from Aldbourne up a dirt track. Aldbourne was where Easy Company, part of the US 101st Airborne Division, depicted in *Band of Brothers*, were based during World War Two. The 1972 story *The Sea Devils* used 19th Century No Man's Land Fort in the sea between Portsmouth and the Isle of Wight. The Royal Navy helped the BBC with *The Sea Devils* and allowed them to use its Whale Island base, HMS Excellent, in Portsmouth as the fictional HMS Seaspite, and also Frazer Gunnery Range. Norris Castle on the Isle of Wight was used as a prison for the dastardly villain, The Master. In the 1973 story *The Three Doctors*, Denham Manor, Denham, Buckinghamshire became UNIT headquarters and some footage of William Hartnell, who was too ill to film in London, was recorded in the garden of his home in Mayfield, Sussex. *The Time Warrior* was filmed at Peckforton Castle in Cheshire (see www.peckfortoncastle.co.uk) and *The Green Death* was filmed at a colliery, now Darran Valley country park in Deri, Glamorgan.

Above: **Sarah-Jane Smith (late Elisabeth Sladen) tries to escape from Linx, a sontaran in *The Time Warrior***

The Fourth Doctor - Tom Baker (1975-1981)

Tom Baker's first story *Robot* was filmed at Wood Norton Hall in Worcestershire and other locations in his first season include: Hound Tor on Dartmoor (*The Sontaran Experiment*) and Wookey Hole caves at Wells in Somerset (*Revenge of the Cybermen*). Scotland was the setting for *The Terror Of The Zygons* but the BBC decided to film much of it in West Sussex. Among the key locations was a pub - The Fox Goes Free at Charlton. Athelhampton House, near Dorchester in Dorset, was the location for the 1976 adventure *The Seeds of Doom* and had also been used for *Sleuth* which stars Michael Caine and Laurence Olivier. Mick Jagger's former home, Stargroves, at East End near Newbury, was used in stories *The Pyramids Of Mars* and *The Image of The Fendahl*. Tom Baker's final scenes in *Logopolis* were filmed at BBC receiving station in Crowsley Park, Berkshire which played the Pharos Project.

The Fifth Doctor - Peter Davison (1982-1984)

Peter Davison, the fifth Doctor, filmed some of his first story Castrovalva at Harrison's Rock, Groombridge, East Sussex, The Visitation at Black Park, near Fulmer in Buckinghamshire (also used for the Baker story *Full Circle,* the Sylvester McCoy story *Battlefield* as well as several *Harry Potter* films, the Bond film *Casino Royale* and *Batman*) and some of *Time-Flight* at Heathrow Airport. Mawdryn Undead was filmed at Middlesex University, Trent Park, Barnet, *The King's Demons* at Bodiam Castle, East Sussex, *The Awakening* at Shapwick in Dorset. Much of the 1984 story *The Resurrection of The Daleks* was filmed in Shad Thames in the London Docklands. Much of the 1983 20th Anniversary show, *The Five Doctors*, was filmed in North Wales (including at a quarry at Blaenau Ffestiniog), although one of Jon Pertwee's sequences in his car, Bessie, was filmed in Denham. Footage of Tom Baker, who didn't take part in the episode, was taken from the 1979 story Shada, which had never been finished because of a BBC strike. In the sequences, the Doctor and his assistant Romana, played by Lalla Ward, are seen punting on the river in Cambridge.

The Sixth Doctor - Colin Baker (1984-1986)

Sixth Doctor Colin Baker had to endure freezing temperatures when he filmed his only Dalek story, *Revelation of the Daleks*, in the snow at Butser Hill near Petersfield. IBM's then futuristic looking UK headquarters at North Harbour, Portsmouth, was used for later scenes also shot in the snow. Blists Hill Victorian Town in Shropshire was used in *The Mark of the Rani*. Camber Sands in East Sussex was used for *The Ultimate Foe* (and had also been used for *The Chase* and the films *Dunkirk* and *Carry On: Follow That Camel)*.

The Seventh Doctor - Sylvester McCoy (1987-1989)

Seventh doctor Sylvester McCoy was supposed to film his 1988 story *Silver Nemesis* at Windsor Castle, but this was blocked by officials so the shoot was switched to Arundel Castle in West Sussex which played Windsor instead. In later scenes Greenwich Gas Works was used as a landing site for a Cyberfleet. Lulworth Cove in Dorset featured in *The Curse of Fenric* and Kew Bridge Steam Museum in Brentford (see www.kbsm.org) was used in *Remembrance of the Daleks*.

The Eighth Doctor – Paul McGann (1996)

Paul McGann made just one appearance as the eighth Doctor in the 1996 adventure *Enemy Within* which was filmed in Canada and San Francisco.

Gavin and Stacey

Barry

The gentle comedy series *Gavin and Stacey* won millions of fans and rightly garnered a string of awards. It has also done much to put the Welsh town of Barry, a few miles from Cardiff, on the map. In the show, which ran from 2007 to 2010, Stacey (Joanna Page) was from Barry and Gavin (Matthew Horne) was from Essex. But the difference in backgrounds and culture didn't hinder their romance, which flourished when they finally met after hitting it off during numerous flirtatious work calls.

Despite being supposedly set in Barry and Essex, location filming for the show was all done in and around Barry, a small town in the Vale of Glamorgan, South Wales. Stacey's house was a private residence on Trinity Street and Gavin's parents' home, supposedly in Billericay, Essex, was in Dinas Powys, the next settlement to Barry. Gavin and his mate Neil's (James Corden) local pub in Essex was actually the Colcot Arms, Colcot Road, Barry. The amusement arcade where Nessa (Ruth Jones) works was at The Western Shelter, Barry Island, Barry's coastal resort and when the family went on a bingo outing during series two those scenes were filmed at Penarth Pier. King's Square in the centre of Barry, outside the Town Hall, was the spot where Nessa decided to try to earn some money as a performance artist. Also featured regularly was Barry Town Station and the branch of Burger King where Gavin's sister worked, again supposedly in Essex, was at Culverhouse Cross near Barry. "We're now having people phoning up saying that they are coming to stay in Barry because of *Gavin and Stacey,*" said Tourism and Marketing Manager Claire Evans. "It is really putting us on the map."

Sat nav references:

Colcot Arms (CF62 8UJ)

Dinas Powys (CF64 4TH)

Town Station (CF62 8AF)

Trinity Street (CF62 7EW)

The Western Shelter (CF62 5TQ)

The Prisoner

Portmeirion

The cult 1960s series *The Prisoner* was filmed at the privately owned Mediterranean-style village of Portmeirion in North Wales. The village, situated at the top of a wooded clifftop, on its own private peninsula overlooking the Traeth Bach estuary and Cardigan Bay, was the inspiration of architect Sir Clough Williams-Ellis who fell in love with the Italian fishing village of Portofino as a young man and resolved to one day create something as charming in Britain. In 1925 he bought a small craggy, wooded peninsula situated between Harlech and Porthmadog. Over the next few years he converted an early Victorian house on the site into a luxury hotel and added cottages. He travelled the country purchasing architecturally interesting but dilapidated buildings, set for demolition, which he brought to Portmeirion and rebuilt.

Above: **It looks like it could be Italy, but actually it's Portmeirion in Wales.**

The village, which became a popular place for visitors including Edward VIII, HG Wells, John Steinbeck and Noel Coward, who wrote his play Blithe Spirit while staying at the hotel, was completed in 1973 and now comprises 50 buildings arranged around a central piazza. Actor Patrick McGoohan discovered Portmeirion while filming an episode of his 60s spy series *Danger Man* in Wales. He realised it was the perfect location for a new series he'd been

Above: **Three views of Sir Clough Williams-Ellis' amazing creation, Portmeirion.**

planning called *The Prisoner,* which showbiz mogul Lew Grade had agreed to finance with a then unheard-of budget of £75,000 an episode.

The series followed the surreal adventures of an ex-spy with no name, just a number - Number Six - marooned in a strange village from which he constantly tries to escape. The 17-part series was a massive hit attracting around 12 million viewers each week. Today the series enjoys cult status and members of The Prisoner Appreciation Society, Six of One, stage a yearly convention at Portmeirion where they re-enact episodes and play the famous Human Chess Game. Portmeirion is open all year round. The hotel was gutted by fire in 1981, but has now been completely renovated and is a splendid place to stay. It has also become a popular venue for weddings. For further information see www.portmeirion-village.com

Sat nav reference:

Portmeirion (LL48 6ER)

Sherlock

Cardiff

Above: **Benedict Cumberbatch as the modern-day Sherlock Holmes.**

Following the huge success of *Doctor Who*, Wales has become a firm favourite for filming and much of this successful series is shot in Cardiff and other parts of South Wales including Swansea and Merthyr Tydfil.

Sherlock is a BBC Wales and Hartswood Films production, co-created by the proven partnership of Steven Moffat and Mark Gatiss and produced by Hartswood's Sue Vertue. It sees the classic Sherlock Holmes tale recreated with a modern and amusing take with actors Benedict Cumberbatch and Martin Freeman in the roles of sleuths Sherlock Holmes and his sidekick Dr John Watson.

Despite being a relatively new show some of the locations used have already become popular tourist attractions with viewers recognising them almost immediately they appeared on screen. For instance, the No Sign Bar in Wind Street, Swansea www. nosignbar.co.uk has become busier than ever, even though it's skillfully disguised in *Sherlock* as Angelo's, an Italian restaurant where Holmes and

Watson eat. Scenes were also shot outside the bar and at one point, bemused passes-by had to be politely moved along as the night shoot threatened to be disrupted.

Production designer Arwel Jones explained that they needed a venue which would feel like a traditional restaurant and was close to an alley and No Sign Bar fitted the bill perfectly. "Plus it's a beautiful building inside," he said.

A stone's throw away, Green Dragon Lane off Wind Street is redesigned into a Westminster street complete with W1 street signs. The road is cobbled and doubles up successfully as a London road.

While some scenes in *Sherlock* are filmed at the Upper Boat studios in Cardiff, home to *Doctor Who*, most are filmed on location. Cardiff University's Main Building proves a useful venue with the production taking over a laboratory in the School of Earth and Social Sciences. The staircases and corridors of the Main Building also feature heavily.

In *The Blind Banker* the National Museum of Wales in Cardiff doubles up as the National Antiquities Museum. Streets used included Newport Road in Cardiff as well as roads in Merthyr Tydfil, all obviously picked to look like London.

But the iconic 221B Baker Street is filmed in London, although round the corner at 185 North Gower Street, W1. The real Baker Street couldn't be used as apart from being extremely busy, there are too many references to Sherlock Holmes which would have had to be disguised.

Above: **Benedict Cumberbatch runs through the streets of Cardiff while filming a scene from *Sherlock*.**

Sat nav references:

**Cardiff University's Main Building
(CF10 3XQ)**

National Museum of Wales (CF10 3NP)

No Sign Bar (SA1 1EG)

Speedy's (NW1 2NJ)

As *Sherlock* is a modern version of the classic, there were discussions as to whether to include the number 221B on Holmes' front door as today there would be doorbells for each flat. In the end it was decided that the sign is too well known to alter so 221B it is.

The actual building used as Holmes' residence is a small sandwich shop called Speedy's which attracted hundreds of new customers just weeks after the first episode of *Sherlock* hit BBC1. "Even now we get tourists taking photographs of the shop, it's amazing!" said an employee. "When the drama was on TV, it was much busier and we were rushed off our feet with customers." The flat above Speedy's in North Gower Street is actually let out to students.

Also in Wales

Above: **The Cavern at Llechwedd Slate Caverns.**

Sat nav reference:

Llechwedd Slate Caverns (LL41 3NB)

Edge of Darkness

The BBC thriller *Edge of Darkness* saw the late Bob Peck play Yorkshire detective Ronald Craven who was investigating the death of his daughter Emma who'd been part of an ecology group which had discovered a secret nuclear plant Northmoor under the Welsh mountains. In reality Northmoor was created by set designers who built an underground complex inside a disused slate mine at Manod, Blaenau Ffestiniog. The entrance used by Craven and CIA officer Darius Jedburgh to enter Northmoor was actually shot at a gold mine at Dolgellau. Llechwedd Slate Caverns at Blaenau Ffestiniog are open to the public. For details telephone 01766 830306 or visit www.llechwedd-slate-caverns.co.uk The conference sequence in the last episode was filmed at Gleneagles in Scotland.

Our Mutual Friend

The Blitz, combined with modern development, caused a headache for the production team preparing to recreate 1860s London for the BBC's 1998 version of *Our Mutual Friend* which starred Paul McGann, Anna Friel, David Morrissey and Keeley Hawes. The major location was a sprawling warehouse on the riverfront overlooking the Thames at Southwark, but there was no genuine site which fitted the bill so a set was built at Cardiff Docks. Elsewhere, a disused stone quarry at Trifil, Wales was used and 17th Century Honington Hall, Shipston-on-Stour, Warwickshire played Mr and Mrs Boffin's home after they gain their wealth. Scenes were also filmed all over London including the English Speaking Union in Charles Street, which played the Veneering's house, the Middle Temple, Lincoln's Inn Fields, Gun Street and Somerset House. The back streets scenes behind the warehouses were filmed at Chatham Dockyard.

Sat nav references:

Chatham Dockyard (ME4 4TZ)

English Speaking Union (W1J 5ED)

Honington Hall (CV36 5AA)

The North West

Bread
Brookside
Coronation Street
Life on Mars
Pride and Prejudice

Bread

Liverpool

Above: **Elswick Street in Liverpool, famous as the setting for *Bread*.**

Elswick Street used to be just another smart row of two-up, two down terraced houses a few yards from the River Mersey in Liverpool. But all that changed when a BBC film crew arrived - and it ended up becoming one of the most famous streets in Britain. As the setting for the comedy series *Bread*, Elswick Street became a popular place for tourists to visit. The big Boswell family lived at Number 30 on screen and grumpy Granddad lived next door at Number 28.

Bread's writer Carla Lane chose Elswick Street to appear in *Bread* because it fitted the image she had of where the Boswells lived and because the road ran down to the River Mersey it suited the scenes she planned to write.

When she writes a script Carla said she actually tells the location manager on the show where she thinks something should be filmed. "I go out on my own and look at places and then I write them in a script," she revealed. "Then the BBC go out and find them from there. I give them more than a hint - I tell them where!"

Brookside

Liverpool

Above: **The Brookside estate.**

In the world of television soaps a great deal of time is spent making sets look just like the real thing. *Coronation Street*, although it looks just like a typical Manchester Street, isn't genuine and the houses in Albert Square, home of *EastEnders*, are fake and don't have backs to them.

Brookside, which ran from 1982 to 2003, was different - the houses seen on screen in the Merseyside soap are very real and were in Brookside Close, a cul-de-sac off Deysbrook Lane on a real estate in the West Derby area of Liverpool. The houses were bought for the programme by *Brookside* creator Phil Redmond and were separated from actual homes nearby by a security barrier.

When characters went through an alleyway between Brookside Close and arrived at Brookside Parade shops it looked as if they'd just walked a few yards. It was just a clever illusion as in actual fact the Brookside Parade, offices and other scenes were filmed five miles away on the site of a former further education college at Childwall.

After the series ended the houses (the six that were seen on screen and seven which were used by the production team as offices) were set to be sold off in the spring of 2008. In March 2008 filming of a horror movie, *Salvage*, starring Shaun Dooley and Neve McIntosh, took place in the close.

Coronation Street

Manchester

Above: **One of the most recognisable sights in Britain...*Coronation Street*.**

Britain's longest-running soap first aired in 1960 and in 2010 celebrated an incredible 50 years with a dramatic live episode and a tram crash causing devastation to the Street and its residents. Set in fictional Weatherfield, *Coronation Street*, or *Corrie* as it is fondly known, is shot mainly on a set at Granada Television's studios in Manchester, although outside locations are also used from time to time. The original Corrie outside set was built in 1969. Until that point, everything had been filmed inside a studio. That set was demolished in 1982 and the current one situated in Quay Street was built at the same time. It was officially opened by The Queen.

The soap's sets change and evolve to meet the needs of the storylines as well as technology. The first sets back in the 60s were long and thin because of fixed lens cameras. Now they can be designed as required; it's simply up to the designers' brief and imagination. As fans of the drama will know, the set incorporates regular fixtures: the Rover's Return pub, a corner shop, a row of terraced houses, two shop units, three houses and a factory – all built in the 80s. Since then, other features have been added from time to time, such as Leanne Battersby's (now Barlow) Italian restaurant which later burnt down, a bar opened by Leanne and Nick Tilsey which unfortunately blew up in the tram crash, a betting shop and Audrey's hair salon, to name a few.

In 1988 the Granada Studios Tour was opened to the public and millions have had the opportunity to walk down the famous cobbles of *Coronation Street*. They were able to stand at the bar in the Rover's Return and peek into Rita's sweet shop, the Kabin, which later became a victim of the tram crash. Unfortunately Granada stopped offering tours in 1999. Some of the off-set locations used by *Corrie* over the years include the stunning Arley Hall and Gardens Estate near Northwich. Open to the public for corporate events and weddings, it has served as an ideal venue for three *Coronation Street* weddings.

Maria Sutherland and the late Liam Connor tied the knot there. Before them, Linda Sykes married Mike Baldwin while Steve McDonald and Karen Philips also used the fabulous grounds for their nuptials. For further information, go to www.arleyhallandgardens.com Sarah Platt and Jason Grimshaw picked the attractive Ryecroft Hall in Audenshaw for their wedding. Other *Corrie* weddings and funerals have been filmed at a church in Prestwich.

Richard Hillman met a watery death in 2003 after driving himself and his family into a canal. This was shot at the Portland Basin Museum, Portland Place, Ashton under Lyne. Actor Brian Capron who played Hillman went on to win a Soap Award for Best Exit later the same year. *Coronation Street* is now set to move to a new location as it has been confirmed that the production will be transferring to Salford Quays, home to the MediaCity UK complex which is due to open in 2012. It will be situated next to the Imperial War Museum North and linked by a new bridge across the Manchester Ship Canal to the rest of the complex. The new *Coronation Street* production centre will include two sound stage buildings, specialist production facilities, offices, dressing rooms and meeting space for production staff.

Sat nav references:

Arley Hall (CW9 6NA)

Portland Basin Museum (OL7 0QA)

Ryecroft Hall (M34 5ZJ)

Life on Mars

Stockport

The first series of *Life on Mars* was screened by the BBC in 2006 and became an instant hit with viewers, going on to win both an Emmy and a BAFTA. Thanks to its quirky storyline and top notch cast – notably John Simm and Philip Glennister – it quickly developed a cult following which has remained loyal, despite only one more series being made the following year. It told the story of DCI Sam Tyler, played by Simm, an officer with the Greater Manchester Police who woke up in 1973 after being hit by a car. He found himself working for Manchester and Salford police force as a DI with a new boss, the maverick DCI Gene Hunt (Glenister).

Described as a 'science-fiction cop drama,' viewers were left wondering whether Tyler was dreaming his new life or whether he really had travelled back in time. Originally, the series was going to be shot in London which then changed to Leeds. Two months before filming began it was settled – Manchester was the chosen location. Tuning in every week while the show was still on air, it was fun for locals to try to recognise various landmarks in and around Manchester, Bury, Oldham, Salford and Stockport and there are several websites dedicated to location spotting.

Below: **Philip Glenister, Liz White and John Simm in a break during filming of *Life on Mars*.**

The police station used by the A Division CID team was actually the back of Stopford House, the home of Stockport Council Offices on Piccadilly. With its

close proximity to the M60, the A6 and the centre of Manchester it made sense that it was chosen by the location team to double as the now iconic cop shop so closely associated with *Life on Mars*.

"It was actually built in 1971 so it fitted perfectly with what we were trying to achieve," said Location Manager Brett Wilson who worked on series one. "We were making out it was the new Manchester police headquarters which in 1973 when *Life on Mars* is set, it would have been." Behind the council building is Stopford Piazza which also featured heavily in the show revamped as a 70s police station car park, complete with Cortinas, bicycles and lampposts. Most of the interior scenes such as the main CID office were shot on a purpose-built set at the BBC's studios in Manchester.

The spot where modern day Sam is hit by a car in the first episode was filmed in a service road underneath the Mancunian Way in Manchester, just off the A6 London Road heading towards Stockport.

The other two main places frequently revisited in *Life on Mars* are Sam's dingy gaffe and the pub, both of which were specially created sets, but fans have always been quick to recognise a whole host of other locations which proved vital to the success of the show.

"We filmed lots of different scenes at the Rochdale Canal at Ancoats," Brett continued. "The opening sequence when Sam comes round in 1973 and is found by a policeman at the car crash site was shot on some waste ground. We also shot the arrest of the villains bursting out of the swimming baths and running along the canal in their trunks by there in another episode." The Grade II listed Victoria Baths in Hathersage Road, Manchester were used in filming at least two episodes. The 100-year-old building was used by the public until 1993 and is renowned for its exquisite architecture, stained glass and ornate tiling. The Turkish Baths within the same complex doubled as the morgue in series two with its Victorian tiling perfect for the purpose, a real morgue at St Thomas's Hospital in Stockport having been used as a morgue in series one.

Victoria Baths are open to the public on the first Sunday of every month between March and October and on National Heritage Days, September 11-14. Telephone 0161 224 2020 for further information or go to www.victoriabaths.org.uk

Many of the industrial back streets used in *Life on Mars* were just off Great Ancoat Street in the Ancoats district, Pollard Street East and Upper Cyrus Street. With its high redbrick walls and run down character, the area was perfect for many of the walking, talking scenes. Mills at Chadderton near Oldham were also used for some exterior shots with interiors filmed at a museum, Queen Street Mill in Burnley.

Sat nav references:

Museum (BB10 2HX)

St Thomas's Hospital, Stockport (SK3 8BL)

Stockport Council Offices (SK1 3XE)

Victoria Baths (M13 0FE)

Above (top): **John Simm as Sam Tyler** *(middle)* **Marshall Lancaster (DC Chris Skelton), Liz White (WPC Annie Cartwright) and Philip Glenister (DCI Gene Hunt) on location.** *(bottom)* **The scene of Sam's accident.**

Pride and Prejudice

Lyme Park

Above (top): **Colin Firth and Jennifer Ehle as Mr Darcy and Elizabeth Bennet in the 1995 BBC adaptation of** *Pride and Prejudice. Above:* **Stunning Lyme Park, one of the largest stately homes in Britain was the main location for** *Pride and Prejudice.*

Sat nav references:

Belton House at Grantham (NG32 2LS)

Brocket Hall (AL8 7XG)

Edgcote Hall (OX17 1AG)

Jane Austen's house (GU34 1SD)

Lord Leycester Hospital (CV34 4BH)

Luckington Court (SN14 6PG)

Lyme Park in Cheshire (SK12 2NR)

Winchester Cathedral (SO23 9LS)

Jane Austen's comedy of manners *Pride and Prejudice* caused a sensation when it was screened on the BBC in September and October 1995 and turned its two lead actors Colin Firth, who played Mr Darcy, and Jennifer Ehle, who played Elizabeth Bennet, into stars. The story centres on Mrs Bennet, played by Alison Steadman, and her pursuit of husbands for her five daughters from the eligible rich young men who come into their social world in 19th Century Hertfordshire.

The BBC's previous version, adapted by Fay Weldon and screened in 1980, had been studio based but the six-part 1995 adaptation, written by award-winning screenwriter Andrew Davies, featured some of Britain's most stunning houses and countryside. For the purposes of filming, Mr Darcy's stunning home Pemberley is quite a distance from Derbyshire, where it is supposed to be, and its exterior shots were actually filmed at beautiful Lyme Park in Cheshire.

Lyme Park, one of the largest houses in the county, is owned by The National Trust and was the home of the Legh family for 600 years. Interior shots of Pemberley were actually filmed closer to where they were set, at late 17th Century Sudbury Hall in Derbyshire, which is again owned by The National Trust. Go to www.nationaltrust.org.uk for details. The Bennet family home Longbourn was actually Luckington Court near Chipping Sodbury in Wiltshire. The house is privately owned and a popular wedding reception venue but is not otherwise open to the public. For further details see www.luckingtoncourt.co.uk

Just 15 miles away is the beautiful village of Lacock, which is also owned by The National Trust, and played Meryton on screen. The village dates back to the 13th Century and its limewashed half-timbered and stone houses also featured in *Harry Potter*, the ITV dramatisations of *Moll Flanders* and *Emma* and the BBC drama *Cranford*.

The Ballroom at Brocket Hall, at Welwyn, Hertfordshire, was used for the main ball held at Netherfield. The Ballroom at Brocket Hall is now an upmarket conference venue. For details see the Brocket Hall website at www.brocket-hall.co.uk The other scenes at Netherfield were filmed at Edgcote Hall near Banbury in Oxfordshire but this is privately owned and not open to the public. Rosings, home of Lady Catherine was played by Belton House at Grantham, Lincolnshire.

Belton, which was built in the late 17th Century, is also now owned by The National Trust and is open for much of the year. For further details go to www.national-trust.org.uk Other scenes were filmed outside the Lord Leycester Hospital in Warwick and the Lambton Inn was in Chapel Street, Longnor, Staffordshire. Jane Austen's real house is now a museum and is located in the village of Chawton near Alton in Hampshire. For details see www.jane-austens-house-museum.org.uk. The writer's grave can be found in Winchester Cathedral.

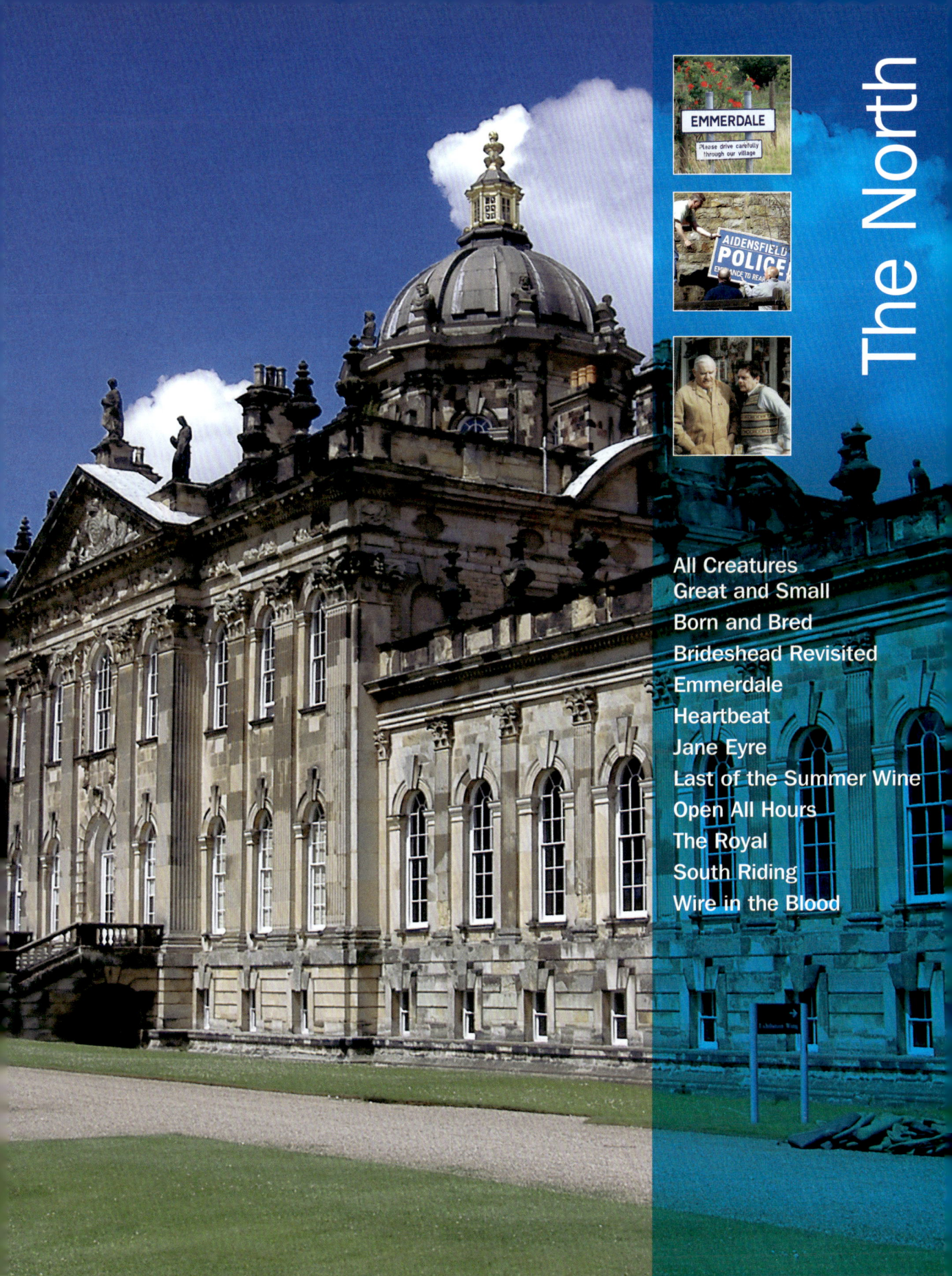

All Creatures
Great and Small
Born and Bred
Brideshead Revisited
Emmerdale
Heartbeat
Jane Eyre
Last of the Summer Wine
Open All Hours
The Royal
South Riding
Wire in the Blood

EMMERDALE
Please drive carefully
through our village

AIDENSFIELD
POLICE

All Creatures Great and Small

Askrigg

All Creatures Great and Small was one of the BBC's biggest drama hits of the 70s and 80s. Based on the novels of vet James Herriot, the series starred Christopher Timothy as Herriot and Robert Hardy as his partner Siegfried Farnon. The real-life surgery on which the books were based was in Thirsk, but the BBC used pretty Askrigg to play fictional Darrowby. Clearly visible in the village is tall Skeldale House which plays the vets' surgery. Next door is a Sykes Store, which plays a sweet shop in the series and across the road is Sticky Ginger café, which is used as the grocer's shop. Nearby is The King's Arms, which plays The Drover's Arms. Not far from Askrigg is Bolton Castle, where James proposed to Helen. It is also used in the BBC series *Ivanhoe* and the feature film *Elizabeth*. See www.boltoncastle.co.uk for more detils. Other locations used in the series include: the market in Hawes, which plays Darrowby Cattle Market, Hardraw church which is Darrowby church and Wensley church, where James and Helen were married.

Right: **James Herriot (Christopher Timothy) and Siegfried Farnon (Robert Hardy) the stars of *All Creatures Great Small*.**

Sat nav references:

Bolton Castle (DL8 4ET)

The King's Arms (DL8 3HQ)

Sticky Ginger café (DL8 3HL)

Wensley church (DL8 4LX)

Born and Bred

Downham

Stunning scenery helped make *Born and Bred* compelling Sunday night viewing between 2002 and 2005. Set in the fictional Lancashire village of Ormston during the 50s, it centred on the relationship between village GP Arthur Gilder (James Bolam) and his city-trained doctor son Tom Gilder, played by Michael French. Much of the family drama was filmed in the real-life village of Downham, near Clitheroe in Lancashire. The village is privately-owned by Lord and Lady Clitheroe and every home is rented by the villagers. What makes it the perfect location for a 50s-set series such as this is the fact that certain trappings of modern day life are banned, making it not too dissimilar to the way it was centuries ago. Ormston Hospital is actually the exterior of three houses within the village.

Right: **The pretty village of Downham played Ormston in the popular BBC series *Born and Bred*.**

Sat nav reference:

Downham (BB7 4BJ)

Brideshead Revisited

Castle Howard

Above: **Stunning Castle Howard, setting for *Brideshead Revisited*.**

When it was first screened the worldwide success of the ITV epic drama *Brideshead Revisited* brought thousands of extra visitors flocking to the series' principal location, Castle Howard in Yorkshire. And even now, two decades after the series was shown in Britain, it still contributes heavily to the number of visitors to Castle Howard, which has been the seat of the Howard family for more than three centuries. *Brideshead Revisited* is often cited as one of ITV's biggest successes - both critically and in terms of ratings - but filming didn't run smoothly. It cost Granada, who made it, more than twice the original budget and a strike by television workers held production up and the crew was disbanded at one point.

When the series finally went into production Granada managed to find a distinguished cast including Laurence Olivier, John Gielgud, Anthony Andrews and Jeremy Irons. The tale of love and passion during the inter-war years was filmed against a backdrop of 18th Century Castle Howard, one of the finest stately homes in Britain, which is set in 1,000 acres of parkland and is as stunning on the outside as it is beautiful inside.

Castle Howard was no stranger to filmmakers. It featured in the 1965 film *Lady L* which starred David Niven, Sophia Loren and Paul Newman and it also featured in a BBC version of *Twelfth Night* in 1978. In 1994 the BBC returned to film the costume drama *The Buccaneers* and in the summer of 2007 a new version of *Brideshead Revisited* went into production starring Michael Gambon and Emma Thompson and much of it was also filmed at Castle Howard. For more details and opening times see www.castlehoward.co.uk

Sat nav reference:

Castle Howard (YO31 7QA)

Emmerdale

Esholt

There's good news and bad news for fans of the ITV soap *Emmerdale*. First the good news: you can visit both villages originally used as Beckindale in the series. The bad news is that you can no longer visit the exterior locations for the show since filming was switched from the village of Esholt to a specially built set on an estate in North Yorkshire in January 1998.

Below: **It looks real - but the *Emmerdale* pictured here is a specially-built set.**

The pretty village of Arncliffe plays the first Beckindale but production was moved in 1976 because producers decided to find somewhere closer to Leeds, where the interior scenes are recorded, because it was quite a trek to Arncliffe. Not only that, Arncliffe had become a Mecca for fans and the village just couldn't cope. Filming was switched to Esholt, just a few miles north west of Leeds, and that in turn became a magnet for lovers of the show, so much so that a special parking site for coaches had to be built nearby.

Then in 1997 Yorkshire Television decided to build a purpose built set on the estate which surrounds historic Harewood House near Leeds, which was once used for the ITV series *Follyfoot*. The success of the series and the pressures of extra episodes made shooting at Esholt too difficult. It had been fine when they only made one episode a week but new episodes heavily increased the workload.

The new set, which took four months to build, isn't an exact replica and Yorkshire Television received quite a few letters when it was first seen on screen because some viewers noticed the change, despite the efforts of expert painters and carpenters.

Unfortunately the set isn't open to the public and a few years ago Yorkshire Television stopped its popular tours of interior sets that it used to run at its Leeds studios. A small consolation is that you can watch a live webcam of the location set. Go to www.itv.com/emmerdale/about/village-webcams

Not every location is on the Harewood Estate set. Creskeld Hall at Arthington doubles as Home Farm and has seen plenty of drama over the years including Frank Tate's death, the murder of Tom King, Zoe blowing up part of the house and Tom being pushed out of his bedroom window. It is now the longest serving location on the programme.

However, Esholt is still worth a visit as you can see the original Woolpack pub in Main Street with a car park behind. The pub, which used to be called The Commercial until the name was changed to fit in with the show and attract tourists, is only ever used in the series for exterior shots.

 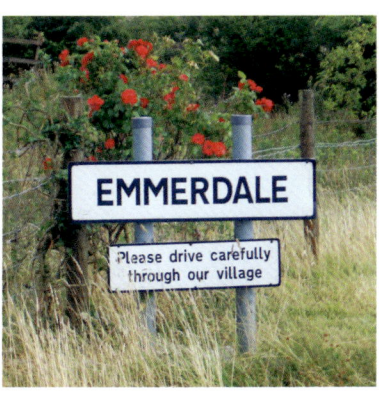 

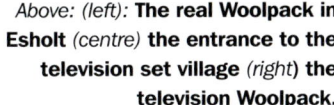

Above: (left): **The real Woolpack in Esholt** *(centre)* **the entrance to the television set village** *(right)* **the television Woolpack.**

A few yards down Main Street, also on the left, is the village hall, which has featured extensively in the series. Just opposite the hall is St Paul's Church which plays Beckindale Church, where Matt married Dolly, Kathy married Jackie and Joe married twice in the show.

On the other side of the church is The Vicarage, which is home for many years to Reverend Donald Hinton, but which in real life has now been turned into three homes. Turning left at the end of Church Lane, follow Chapel Lane for a short while until you find Cunliffe Lane.

Turn into it and you'll see Bunker's Hill, which was better known on screen as Dem dyke, until it was 'destroyed' on screen in the 1993 plane crash storyline. On screen, Number Six plays Seth Armstrong's house and Number Three houses Nick, Elsa and Alice. And - just a reminder - the houses are homes to real people not connected with *Emmerdale*.

Sat nav references:

Creskeld Hall (LS21 1NT)

St Paul's Church (BD17 7RA)

Woolpack pub (BD17 7QZ)

Market scenes have been filmed in the nearby town of Otley, which plays Hotten in the series and other places that are used include: Almscliffe Crag, Brimham Rocks, Plumptom Rocks, Valley Gardens, Harrogate and Golden Acre Park, Leeds. In addition Wakefield, Leeds and Morley town halls are used for courtroom scenes.

Heartbeat

Goathland

Right: **PC Rob Walker (Jonathan Kerrigan), district nurse Carol Cassidy (Lisa Kay) and PC Phil Bellamy (Mark Jordon).**

When the residents of picturesque North Yorkshire village Goathland learned this 60s-set drama had been axed after 18 years, they went into shock. For not only had *Heartbeat* been a Sunday night telly favourite for so long but it kept a healthy stream of visitors coming to the village, so boosting its economy.

At the start of the series in 1992, former *EastEnders* actor Nick Berry played London police constable Nick Rowan who quit his inner city beat to take a job as a rural village bobby along with his doctor wife Kate, played by Niamh Cusack. Inevitably over the many years the series ran, members of the cast changed and latterly it was Joe Mason (Joe McFadden) who pounded the rural beat along with PC Don Weatherby (Rupert Ward-Lewis).

Whether or not the coach loads of excited *Heartbeat* fans who tipped up at Goathland still make the trek now new episodes are no longer being made, remains to be seen. All the beautiful locations are still there of course and can be appreciated on the show's repeats both in Britain and abroad.

Below: **A view of picturesque Goathland.**

There's plenty to see in Goathland and when you drive through the village you'll reach a right-hand bend and the stone house on your right is Glendale House, which played Kate Rowan's surgery in the series. The house was built in 1875 by Edward Fuller Sewell, an uncle of Anna Sewell, author of the novel *Black Beauty*.

It's a Victorian stone-built residence and occupies a prime position in the centre of the picturesque village, overlooking the common, where sheep graze right outside the garden gate. Its owners, Keith and Sandra

Above (top): **Glendale House, which was used as Kate Rowan's surgery and is now a B&B** *(above)* **Members of the crew dress the set.**

Sat nav references:

Aidensfield Stores (YO22 5LX)

Brow House Farm (YO22 5NP)

Glendale House (YO22 5AN)

Goathland Hotel (YO22 5LY)

Goathland Primary School (YO22 5ND)

Simmonds, offer reasonably priced bed and breakfast. For details see www.glendalehouse.co.uk

Sandra said the impact of *Heartbeat* on Goathland was hugely positive and while there, the production team bent over backwards to minimise disruption to the village. "We've had visitors from as far afield as Tasmania, Russia and even Peru because of *Heartbeat*," she added.

Over at Brow House Farm, the location for Claude Greengrass' farm, farmers John and Keith Jackson have opened up some of their fields as a campsite. The site was up and running before *Heartbeat* began but once the series was broadcast, tourists were even more keen to stay. In fact at one point business was so good, the Jacksons gave over another field to campers to cope with the demand. Facilities offered to campers and caravanners include running water, a shower and toilets and electricity hook-up points. Bookings can be made by telephoning 01947 896274.

Real life Goathland Garage appeared in the series as Scripp's Garage and across the road from it is The Goathland Hotel which played the local pub, The Aidensfield Arms. You'll also see the shops which feature in the series including the real post office which played the post office in the show and Aidensfield Stores, run by Phil and Ros Hopkinson, which remained the same on the outside whether filming was taking place or not and sells a range of Heartbeat merchandise. See www.aidensfieldstores. co.uk for further details. "*Heartbeat* has been great for business," said Phil. "And the show's popularity means we get people here from all over the world."

The Goathland Primary School featured heavily in the show when Nick Rowan's second wife Jo Weston was in the series and in real life the school benefited from a donation from Yorkshire Television which helped kit the pupils out in new school uniforms. A private house, Brereton Cottage on Brereton Corner played the police house and also not open to the public is a farm which played Peggy Armstrong and David Stockwell's farm.

We don't often see the exterior of the police station in later episodes, but in older ones, the former police station in Courthouse Street, Otley, about 75 miles from Goathland, was used. When Heartbeat began most scenes – both interior and exterior - were filmed in Goathland but later, most interior scenes were shot at a studio built inside a former mill near Leeds, which was once used as the studio for filming interiors for *Emmerdale*. Sets of Ashfordly Police Station, the doctor's surgery and the pub were built there as it proved cheaper and easier to film interior scenes there.

Jane Eyre

Bakewell

An all-star cast helped make BBC's 2006 glossy adaptation of Charlotte Bronte's *Jane Eyre* one of the most popular television remakes of this much-loved classic, winning both an Emmy and a BAFTA the following year.

Dovedale, the rocky National Trust land in the Derbyshire Dales, is featured in the opening episode where Rochester and Jane initially meet in the mist. Rochester's home, Thornfield, is in fact Haddon Hall, a stunning medieval castle in Bakewell, Derbyshire which is owned by Lord and Lady Edward Manners. Some of the scenes supposedly set at Thornfield were in fact shot at a studio miles away and at another building.

North Haddon Hall has featured in a number of other television shows and films, including the BBC's *The Prince and the Pauper* and more recently, the movie remake of *Pride and Prejudice*, starring Keira Knightley and Matthew MacFadyen. In particularly dramatic scenes, Thornfield is seen burning through the night, thanks to the use of special effects. During filming the local fire brigade received dozens of calls from worried locals who believed Haddon Hall was genuinely on fire. For further information go to www.haddonhall.co.uk If you're planning on visiting Bakewell, why not take in the village of Hathersage in Derbyshire which is just an eight mile drive north. Once renowned for its milling industries, the area is now the perfect place to walk and climb as it is overlooked by moors and gritstone edges, including the well-known Stanage Edge. Ruth Wilson's Jane is seen standing here in episode four.

Below: **Ilam Park, one of the settings for *Jane Eyre*.**

Charlotte Bronte visited Hathersage in 1845 and took the name Eyre for her novel's heroine from the local family. It is believed that she based Thornfield, the house from where Mrs Rochester jumps from the roof to her death, on North Lees Hall, an Elizabethan manor house which is situated about a mile north of Hathersage. In the book she describes it as: "three storeys high, of

Above: **Beautiful Dovedale in the Derbyshire Dales.**

proportions not vast, though considerable: a gentleman's manor house." This description fits North Lees Hall to a tee. The BBC certainly thought so and used the Hall as Thornfield (along with Haddon Hall as mentioned earlier). The property is now owned by the Peak District National Park Authority and is open to the public for one weekend in September. Telephone Yorkshire Bridge Inn Ltd for further information on 01433 651361.

If you stood on Carhead Rocks above North Lees Hall and looked behind you, you'd see Overstones Farm, which doubled as Rivers Cottage.

Much of the early part of *Jane Eyre* takes place at Lowood School and for this, the BBC opted for Bolsover Castle which provided some of the school's interiors. Built in the 12th Century, it is now in the care of English Heritage. It also served as Jane's school during her early years when she was played by the young actress Georgie Henley, while some of her fellow pupils were played by youngsters from local drama school, the Ripley Academy. The Riding House at Bolsover Castle was transformed into the school's dormitory. Wingfield Manor at South Wingfield, near Alfreton, Derbyshire was used as Thornfield after the great fire wreaks havoc. A ruined country mansion, it was once the home of one of Britain's wealthiest men, Lord Ralph Cromwell, having built it for himself in 1439. It's particularly fascinating when you learn that Mary Queen of Scots was held prisoner here three times in the 1500s. The building has remained unoccupied since 1772 and is now owned by English Heritage. To arrange to visit or learn more about its history see www.english-heritage.org.uk

Ilam Hall at Ashbourne, a 19th Century Victorian Gothic manor house, and its surrounding gardens are managed by the National Trust and are now used as a youth hostel, tea rooms and car park. The hall doubled up as the exterior of Lowood School. Situated in the village of Ilam, it is to be found between Buxton and Ashbourne. Tel 0870 7705876 to book the youth hostel. For more details about the house see www.nationaltrust.org.uk Another Trust property, Kedleston Hall, an 18th Century mansion north-west of Derby, features in the scene where Rochester meets his future wife Bertha. The mansion is renowned for its art treasures and one particular room, Caesar's Hall, is transformed into a Caribbean setting where a lavish dinner is staged. Go to www.nationaltrust.org.uk to learn more about this stunning building and for details of opening times.

Sat nav references:

Bolsover Castle (S44 6PR)

Haddon Hall (DE45 1LA)

Ilam Hall (DE6 2AZ)

Kedleston Hall (DE22 5JH)

Wingfield Manor (DE55 7NH)

Last of the Summer Wine

Holmfirth

Over more than 30 years Roy Clarke's gentle comedy *Last of the Summer Wine* has given the Yorkshire town of Holmfirth the sort of publicity that tourism industry chiefs can usually only dream of. The series ran from 1973 to 2010 and helped put the town firmly on the tourist map and showed off the full beauty of the Pennine countryside. Each year thousands of fans of the BBC comedy flock to Holmfirth to see for themselves the real-life setting for the show. Now the show is no longer being made, time will tell whether or not interest in visiting Holmfirth diminishes.

If you are planning a visit, a good first port of call - particularly after a long drive - must be the cafe used as Sid's Cafe in the series, latterly, run on-screen by Ivy. A former paint store for a nearby hardware shop, the cafe looks much the same off-screen as on and the BBC.

Local man Colin Frost ran the cafe with his wife Maggie for 15 years until 2006 when it was taken over by sisters Ailsa and Laura Booth. "The popularity of *Last of the Summer Wine* goes right round the world," said Ailsa. "We've had customers from as far afield as Australia and New Zealand and even people from Finland."

Above (left): **Nora Batty's famous steps** *(centre)* **the iconic Sid's Cafe** *(right)* **The White Horse at Jackson Bridge.**

Former owner Colin Frost now runs tours of filming locations. See www.summerwine.tv for details. No trip to Holmfirth is complete without taking a peek at Nora Batty's famous house. It is just a short walk from the cafe along Hollowgate. At the end of Hollowgate is a bridge and from it you can see Nora's house, Number 28 Scarfold and below is the door to Compo's flat, which now houses The Summerwine Exhibition, run by Sue and Chris Gardner. The couple also own The Wrinkled Stocking Tea Room next door at Number 30, another good place to take a break. It is open for most of the year. See www.wrinkledstocking.co.uk for details.

Nora's house is now available as a holiday cottage. Businessman Neil Worthington bought the house a few years ago and planned to expand his graphic design and advertising business at Numbers 24 and 26 into it. But he

Sat nav references:

The Butcher's Arms (HD9 1TE)

The Cafe (HD9 2DG)

The White Horse Inn (HD9 1LY)

The Wrinkled Stocking Tea Room (HD9 2JS)

changed his mind and decided to open the world-famous house for self-catering accommodation instead. For booking details see: www.nora-batty.co.uk The house even contains some Nora Batty props and as Neil's website says it is "A shrine to Nora Batty, fully furnished, as only Nora would approve. Tastefully decorated in keeping with the overall Nora Batty Experience." Neil said: "We're quite unique – there aren't many film sets you can actually stay in."

While in the area you might like to call in for a pint at The White Horse Inn at Jackson Bridge which appeared in the show many times. See www.thewhitehorsejacksonbridge.co.uk for details. Behind the pub at Jackson Bridge is the private house which doubled as home for Cleggy, Pearl and Howard. From Jackson Bridge you may like to drive to Hepworth where you'll find another of the trio's locals, The Butcher's Arms. See www.thebutchersarmshepworth.co.uk for details.

Left: **Nora Batty dishes out justice to Compo, Foggy and Clegg.**

Open All Hours

Doncaster

You won't find Arkwright's grocers shop open all hours if you go to Number 15, Lister Avenue in Doncaster. Nor will you be able to buy a p-p-p-packet of cornflakes or a l-l-l-loaf of bread. But you might be able to get your hair cut! For the shop that plays stuttering Arkwright's shop in the highly successful BBC comedy *Open All Hours*, and became Britain's best-known shop front, is actually a hair salon.

The BBC picked the shop because it had a traditional double front and fitted the bill perfectly as Arkwright's old-style corner shop. So for three weeks a year, for four years, the BBC rolled their camera equipment into the street and moved owner Helen Ibbotson's hairdryers and curlers out of her shop. The BBC covered up Helen's Beautique sign with a board bearing Arkwright's name and dressed up the front of the shop with stocks of food. And, of course, they painted details of Arkwright's bargain of the week on the window.

"It was never a real inconvenience," Helen explained. "I used to shut down when they were here. The BBC used to pay me very nicely - a bit more than the hairdressing. So it paid for a holiday, which was very handy." Helen got another bonus too - free vegetables! After filming had ended the BBC often used to give her Arkwright's vegetables. "They gave me a lot of the stuff and I made wine with the parsnips and carrots," she said.

Helen had good memories of the show's two stars Ronnie Barker, who plays stuttering Arkwright, and David Jason, who plays Granville. She said: "David was a very funny man and nice to get on with. Ronnie was very nice too but a bit more serious than David - but still very jolly. People seemed to like them in the street. They always used to get a good crowd when they were filming."

Above (left): **Ronnie Barker and David Jason as Arkwright and Granville on location in Doncaster** *(right)* **the shop as it is now.**

Across the road from Helen's shop is Number 34 which played the home of Arkwright's love, nurse Gladys Emmanuel (Lynda Baron). After it was used for the first series the then owner altered the look of the front of the house and when the BBC came to make the next series they decided it no longer suited them. So filming was switched to Number 32 next door - and the BBC hoped no one would notice. In 2006 Doncaster council chiefs put forward a new development plan for parts of the town which many people believed could see areas including Lister Avenue facing demolition. A petition and campaign have been set up against the plan, although councillors accused campaigners of scaremongering and said nothing had been finalised.

Sat nav reference:

Hair Salon (DN4 8AS)

The Royal

Scarborough

When *Heartbeat* came to an end in 2010, sadly so did its spin-off *The Royal* which was filmed in the seaside town of Scarborough and centred around the fictional St Aiden's Royal Free Hospital. Exterior shots for the series, which starred Robert Daws as Dr Gordon Ormerod and Amy Robbins as Dr Jill Weatherill, were shot outside Red Court apartments in Holbeck Road.

Interior scenes were filmed in a studio, but other locations that were used for the series, include Goathland and Calverley. Scarborough has been featured many times on TV and in films with appearances in *Little Voice*, Rik Mayall Presents: *Dancing Queen* and *Dalziel and Pascoe*.

South Riding

Yorkshire

Andrew Davies's three-part adaptation of the novel by Winifred Holtby was screened by BBC One in February 2011 and was set against a stunning Yorkshire landscape.

The story, set in the 1930s, sees the arrival from London to the South Riding, of career woman Sarah Burton (Anna Maxwell Martin) to take up the post of headmistress at a high school for girls. Following the death of Sarah's fiancé in the First World War, she's given up on marriage and motherhood but she hasn't banked on meeting Robert Carne (David Morrissey), a man whose family have farmed the South Riding for centuries and who has his own troubles...

The production was based in Leeds and interiors were shot in various areas across the region. For example, the interior of girls' school, Kiplington High, was a disused infants' school on the outskirts of Leeds while the exterior was actually a completely different school – All Saints Primary in Bradford which looked similar.

Above: **The beautiful scenery at Skipsea.**

"All the coastal locations used were at Skipsea, east Yorkshire," said location manager Luc Webster. "Because the site where the Shacks were, was the original site she (Holtby) based her novel we shot there. It was actually like a shanty town, along the cliff tops. The Shacks were recreated on the disused Acaster Malbis Airfield, north Yorkshire (where the Holly family's railway carriage was also built) and the interior of the carriage was recreated at the studio in Leeds."

A large privately owned mansion house 10 miles outside Durham doubled up as Robert Carne's home while fans of the drama may be interested to learn that the character's stable yard actually forms part of another property entirely, a stunning Grade II listed mansion called Rise Hall. The magnificent house belongs to television presenter Sarah Beeny and in fact her trials and tribulations in restoring it were featured on Channel Four's *Beeny's Restoration Nightmare*. It is now available for weddings and other events. Visit www.risehall.com to learn more.

The production crew found themselves on the road a good deal during the shoot and in fact travelled to an impressive 35 locations in 44 days. Naturally we can't list each and every one here but viewers may recognise the seafront in Bridlington, some areas in Harrogate where many scenes were shot and private homes were used as well as the Great Central Railway in Loughborough www.gcrailway.co.uk Many of the council scenes were filmed at Morley Town Hall in Leeds as was the Floral Hall Concert.

Sat nav references:

All Saints Primary (BD5 0NG)

Great Central Railway (LE11 1RW)

Morley Town Hall (LS27 9DY)

Rise Hall (HU11 5BL)

Wire in the Blood

Newcastle

Above: **The city of Newcastle was used as the setting for *Wire In The Blood*.**

This gritty crime series was screened on ITV between 2002 and 2009, finally being axed due to high production costs. It remains hugely successful however as it is sold in over 30 countries around the world. Made by Coastal Productions, *Wire in the Blood* was filmed in and around Newcastle and starred Robson Green as clinical psychologist Dr Tony Hill who got inside the head of killers in order to help police solve bizarre crimes. He worked closely on a range of often gruesome cases with Detective Inspector Alex Fielding, played by Simone Lahbib, who took over in series four from Detective Chief Inspector Carol Jordan, played by Hermione Norris.

Newcastle itself was never mentioned in *Wire in the Blood*, which is supposedly based in the fictional metropolis of Bradfield. "This is taken to be 'somewhere up north,' and is very definitely not Newcastle, or anywhere else for that matter," said Location Manager Gareth Williams.

Anything which could identify Newcastle was studiously avoided by Coastal, Gareth revealed. "The city has got loads of wonderful locations but we don't want people to visually tire of the north east. "As fans of the drama will know, it is a dark show and much of it was filmed during the winter for obvious reasons. A large part of *Wire in the Blood* was filmed on a purpose-built set, home to the police station, in Heaven, Newcastle. For the first three seasons, the inside of the police station was filmed in the former Bank of England in the centre of Newcastle. The building has an interesting history – it was the second biggest bullion store in the country outside of London – but the set itself wasn't felt to be especially interesting.

The set used for the final season of *Wire in the Blood* began to take shape in series four when the production team came across a former Rolls Royce switch gear factory on the Team Valley. With its ranks of grey steel shelving and steel staircases, it was considered ideal police station material.

Unfortunately, after series four, the building wasn't available any longer so Gareth bought all of the steel staircases and grey shelving which were moved to another warehouse in Wallsend, Newcastle. The designer for series five remodelled the set using the props and made it even more camera friendly. That was the blueprint for the set used for series six, although in the interim, the production lost the warehouse. Early in 2008, Gareth was sent to find a similar warehouse and managed to track one down in Heaven which is where the set is now standing, getting dusty and waiting to be reused.

Sat nav reference:

Bank of England (NE1 6SU)

Scotland

Doctor Finlay

Auchtermuchty

Auchtermuchty became the fictional Scottish town of Tannochbrae in the 1993 series of *Doctor Finlay* by chance when the series' producer Peter Wolfes drove through the town on his way to view another possible location. Many buildings in the town centre, The Cross, were used for filming and The Forest Hills Hotel become a temperance hotel, The Salvation. The Post Office appeared regularly although it was turned into The Flying Dutchman pub.

Auchtermuchty Town Hall, which was the town's police station many years ago and still has the old cells, reverted back to its former role to play Tannochbrae Police Station. The town's council offices doubled as the local bank and the entrance to the library was altered to fit the 1950s style and was used as Tannochbrae library. What was missing from Auchtermuchty was the surgery, Arden House, and that was because it wasn't in the town. In fact it was more than 70 miles away on a country estate just outside Glasgow. The original 60s series *Doctor Finlay's Casebook* was filmed in Callander but producers decided not to use it for the 1993 series because it had become too busy.

Sat nav references:

Auchtermuchty Town Hall (KY14 7AP)

The Forest Hills Hotel (KY14 7AP)

Post Office (KY14 7AR)

Hamish Macbeth

Plockton

The sleepy village of Plockton on the north west coast of Scotland found fame in the late 1990s as the fictional village of Lochdubh, home beat of PC Hamish Macbeth, played by Robert Carlyle, who has gone on to become a major film star. To find the right location to play Lochdubh for the BBC series, the show's producers toured 1,200 miles of the west coast of Scotland. "As soon as we saw Plockton we knew it was perfect," recalled Producer Deidre Keir. "It's extraordinarily beautiful, it's not on a main road and it has the same kind of close-knit community as Lochdubh."

Although remote, Plockton is just over the sea from Skye and attracts visitors from all over the world. It lies in a sheltered inlet, surrounded by heather-clad mountains and with views across Loch Carron, the gulf stream climate accounts for unexpected palm trees which fringe its harbour and seals are a common sight in its calm waters. Before the BBC team arrived in the village en masse Deirdre and her team made sure the locals were happy with the prospect of a 70-strong film unit arriving. Plockton's newsagent Edmund McKenzie agreed to move his shop into the sailing club next door for three months so that his premises could be used by the BBC and converted into the Lochdubh general store. Visitors to Plockton were constantly surprised to find the village shop was faked and stocked only with props. The whitewashed house chosen to be both Hamish's home and the police station is a holiday home owned by a Glasgow doctor. On one occasion a family from London who had pre-booked a week's holiday arrived to find their cottage adorned with a blue lamp and bars at the window and police cell where a bedroom used to be.

High Road

Luss

Sat nav references:

Coffee Club (G84 8AD)

Highland Arts Gift Shop (G83 8NZ)

Youth Hostel (G83 8RB)

The Scottish soap, which ran from 1980 to 2003, was filmed in Luss on the banks of Loch Lomond where the pretty village doubled as fictional Glendarroch. The big house in the series was actually the Youth Hostel at nearby Arden, which can be seen from the main road and the hostel's annexe nearby played the Glendarroch Hotel in a series, although the interior shots are recorded in the studio. Anyone wanting to stay at the hostel must be a member of the Youth Hostel Association.

In Luss itself, filming took place at the Highland Arts Gift Shop, which played Blair's Store, outside several cottages, at the church and at the manse. The ferry featured regularly and we often saw characters walking along the beach and on the pier. A farm at nearby Glenfruin was also featured. The nearby town of Helensburgh also appeared in the series for lots of shop scenes and the Coffee Club in Colquhoun Square appeared regularly.

Monarch of the Glen

Loch Laggan

Thanks to its views of the glorious Scottish Highlands and acres of breathtaking scenery, *Monarch of the Glen* became unmissable Sunday night viewing between 2000 and 2005, with seven successful series making it one of the most popular television shows to come out of Scotland.

Even now, it is repeated all over the world and fans still make their way to stunning Loch Laggan, 16 miles south west of Newtonmore where much of the series was filmed, to catch a glimpse of all the landmarks which made Monarch so memorable.

The gorgeous setting for the fictional village of Glenbogle, with its mixture of eccentric and somehow innocent characters, was the village of Laggan and the splendid Glenbogle Castle, inhabited by Richard Briers' character Laird Hector Bogle, was played by the privately-owned Ardverikie House. The house can be seen – and photographed – from across the loch on the main Newtonmore to Fort William Road and indeed, many fans of the show still visit Ardverikie when they're in the area, despite it being off-limits to the general public.

"We always know where Monarch is showing at a given time depending on the nationality of our visitors," said Robert Noble, former manager of the Ardverikie House estate. "We get lots of Australian tourists for example and

Right: **Privately-owned Ardverikie House, which was used as Glenbogle Castle in *Monarch of the Glen*.**

Norwegians. It's always being repeated somewhere. We can't stop people wandering on to the estate but we do ask that they respect the privacy of the family and others who live here." During its heyday, Monarch brought a buzz to Ardverikie and Laggan as endless crew and cast members arrived to begin filming for several months at a time.

Laggan locals and residents from a little further afield in the Badenoch areas of Newtonmore, Kingussie and Kincraig and further still, Strathspey (the area from Aviemore northwards), which were areas also used to shoot scenes, often became extras, boosting morale no end and ensured everyone was happy with the whole *Monarch of the Glen* experience.

"The production company (Ecosse) were given exclusive rights to the main part of Ardverikie House between February and October each year in order to film *Monarch*," Robert continued. The family were able to use a wing during this period which had been renovated for them; then they moved back into the house once the film crews had left.

"It was obviously a very busy time while filming was taking place because there were about a 100 cast and crew and this of course meant it was very good for the local economy. They had to have accommodation and as there wasn't enough room on the estate for everyone, the local guest houses did very well. Again the local shops were very pleased of the extra custom too as were the pubs. All in all, *Monarch* was very good for the area and surrounding locations."

The Gate Lodge, a holiday cottage belonging to the estate was often featured on *Monarch*. With its turret and picturesque setting at the entrance to the grounds, it is an ideal honeymoon retreat and is nearly always booked up months, if not years ahead. Another larger, self-catering estate property, Gallovie, doubled up as a bed and breakfast in the final series of *Monarch*. Again, it is possible to stay here – if you're lucky enough to book early.

Right: **Richard Briers, Alastair Mackenzie and Susan Hampshire, the stars of *Monarch of the Glen*.**

There are also a further three self-catering properties available to rent on the Ardverikie estate. For further information, go to www.ardverikie.com

The loch itself was also a feature of *Monarch*. A plane was sunk in its waters in one episode and of course, tragically Hector drowned in it. Susan Hampshire's character Molly was an artist and you may be interested to learning 'her' paintings were actually creations of a Newtonmore artist, David Fallows.

Local hotels often doubled up as Glenbogle premises and have become popular tourist spots as a result. For example, The Glen Hotel in Newtonmore, the car park of which sometimes popped up in *Monarch*, is worth a visit. Go to www.theglenhotel.co.uk to make a booking.

As an impressive seven series were filmed in all, it's not surprising that a vast number of locations featured in *Monarch*, certainly too many to mention here, although the main ones have been highlighted. For further details go to www.monarchcountry.com

Sat nav references:

Ardverikie House (PH20 1BX)

The Glen Hotel (PH20 1DD)

Taggart

Glasgow

In 2011, after 28 years ITV1 decided not to commission any further episodes of *Taggart* – which was the longest-running detective drama on television anywhere in the world - after a drop in viewing figures in the UK. However, the show remains hugely popular in Scotland so Scottish Television which makes it, wants it to continue.

The late Mark McManus stars as DCI Jim Taggart in the pilot episode screened in 1983 and he continues in the role as the tough, experienced cop until 1994 when he sadly passed away.

Taggart's young and relatively inexperienced side-kick was DS Peter Livingstone, played by Neil Duncan, while his boss, Superintendent Jack McVitie is played by Iain Anderson. In 1987, Mike Jardine (James MacPherson) joins the show and four years later, Jackie Reid – Blythe Duff – replaces Livingstone as Taggart's right-hand officer.

It was a severe shock to the whole cast and crew when Mark McManus died suddenly in the middle of filming and his absence had to be explained away in the script. Jardine has already been elevated to DI and he is joined by his own side-kick, DC Stuart Fraser, played by Colin McCredie. DI Robbie Ross played by John Michie joins the team in 1998.

Above: **The late Mark McManus, the original star of *Taggart*.**

In 2002, actor Alex Norton's character DCI Matt Burke replaces Mike Jardine (killed off when MacPherson decided to leave) so today, Norton, McCredie, Michie and Duff are the four current stars of the show which is screened all over the world.

Taggart is filmed primarily in the Glasgow area, although as you can imagine, in almost three decades, literally hundreds of locations have been used so it would be a near impossible task to try and list each and every one of them here!

But certainly when you tune in, it's possible to instantly spot some well-known attractions such as the famous St Andrews Suspension Bridge which is located in the corner of Glasgow Green, furthest from the City Centre. The Bridge links Glasgow Green with St Adelphi Street on the other side of The Clyde.

Then there's Central Station, Glasgow's main railway station; The People's Palace which was built in 1898 as a cultural centre for the city's workers; The Winter Gardens, a large conservatory on the back of the Palace; Glasgow School of Art; George Square; Barrowland where a street market takes place every week; Scott Street, Buchanan Street and a string of restaurants and cafes.

Exterior scenes for the police station are filmed at the Colville Building, North Portland Street, which is part of Strathclyde University. The main police station and incident room featured in every episode are actually purpose-built sets and these have been constructed in around a dozen or so locations since *Taggart* began. An industrial unit at Polmadie is the latest set to be used.

Over the years, the use of new technology crept on to the set and plasma screens and some computer generated graphics were all part of making *Taggart* a 21st Century police drama.

Donald Mackinnon, who was Location Manager for several episodes of *Taggart* said pretty much the whole of Glasgow is used to film *Taggart* and the city has been the perfect backdrop, evolving alongside the show.

"We film pretty much all around Glasgow," said Donald. "We use the city as a backdrop and have evolved alongside it. We feature the university quite a lot, the West End, many of the city's shipyards and of course the river as a lot of people have been bumped off and later found there!

"We've had a few funerals as well. Some years ago when one of our major characters (Jardine) was killed off, he was buried at the Necropolis which is one of the most famous cemeteries in Glasgow." In fact the Necropolis is part of Glasgow's 'Heritage Trail,' and is one of the most significant cemeteries in Europe, attracting visitors from all over the UK and abroad.

Sat nav references:

Colville Building (G1 1XN)

Glasgow School of Art (G3 6RQ)

Necropolis (G4 0UZ)

The People's Palace (G40 1AT)

Railway Station (G1 3SL)

Bergerac
Ballykissangel
The Invisibles

Jersey, Ireland & Northern Ireland

Bergerac

Jersey

For an island just nine miles long, with a population of just 83,000, there were an awful lot of crimes committed on Jersey during the 1980s - well on screen at least. But far from putting visitors off the success of the BBC detective series *Bergerac* brought visitors flocking to the island. The Jersey tourist authorities were delighted by the free publicity and they even hired the series' star, John Nettles, who played Triumph Roadster-driving Sergeant Jim Bergerac, to appear in their advertisements.

Most of the 45 square-mile island got a look in at some point during the series' 10-year run, which began in 1981. Lots of the locations used for the series are easy to see but not even a super-sleuth like Jim Bergerac could find the attractive stone cottage and farm that played his home in the first few series. For it was located in Queen's Valley in the east of the island and is now under hundreds of thousands of gallons of water as the whole valley was flooded in 1992 to make the new Queen's Valley Reservoir.

Jim's ex-father-in-law, millionaire Charlie Hungerford, played by Terrance Alexander, lived in a luxury home, portrayed by two different houses. The first was Noirmont Manor, a beautiful house overlooking Belcroute Bay. The second was Windward House, which is private, and overlooks St Brelade's Bay. The Jersey Police Headquarters Jim worked from, the Bureau Des Estranges (Department for non Residents) is supposed to be in St Helier but is actually, Haute de la Garenne, a former childrens' home in the Parish of St Martin's in the east of the Island, which the BBC also used as a production base during filming. In reality, there is no such police department. Haute de la Garenne, now a centre for activity holidays, became the focus of a major police investigation in early 2008.

Above: **A young John Nettles as Jim Bergerac.** *Below:* **One of Jersey's many stunning beaches.** *Opposite:* (top) **Mont Orgueil Castle** (bottom) **An aerial view of Seymour Tower on Jersey's East Coast**

One of Jim's regular contacts was Diamante Lil, played by actress Mela White, who ran a restaurant and bar called The Royal Barge. In real life the restaurant was The Old Court House at St Aubin, a popular venue for both locals and visitors. Only the exterior is used for filming - the interior of The Royal Barge was a set built inside the Forum cinema in St Helier. Around the island dozens of places were used for filming the series. For example, the Round Tower, the most southerly German wartime fortification at Noirmont Point was used for an action sequence when a stunt man is thrown from the top of the tower to the rocks below after a fight.

The Norman Church of St Brelade, which dates back to the 11th Century, and its churchyard were used many times for weddings and funerals and the church hall played the headquarters of a dastardly medium in one episode. St Ouen's Manor, a private house which dates back to the 13th Century, was used repeatedly in the series in various guises as an art gallery and museum, as a French chateau, as the headquarters of a neo-fascist and as home to an eccentric millionaire, who was robbed by the ice maiden, Philippa Vale, played by Liza Goddard.

Beau Port, an attractive secluded beach, featured in an episode where Charlie Hungerford planned to build a huge hotel complex on the valley leading to it and cover the whole bay with a retractable glass dome. Needless to say, like many of Charlie's wilder ideas, it didn't happen, on or off screen. Mont Orgueil Castle was used just once in *Bergerac* in an episode about a German film star, played by Warren Clarke, who was making a movie in Jersey about the wartime German occupation. Jim later has a fight with the character and that took place on a large German bunker on the southern headland at St Ouen's Bay.

The beach at St Ouen's was featured many times and in one episode two young surfers found the body of a skin-diver there. Not far away, at St Mary's, on the road from St Ouen to Trinity, is the Ecole Elementaire, which played the school of Jim's daughter Kim. John Nettles ran into trouble with the real Jersey police during the filming of one episode when Jim chased a villain across St Brelade's Bay on a jet ski. Afterwards he was ticked off by an angry officer.

Like viewers, John Nettles fell in love with Jersey while filming *Bergerac*, and used to have a home there. He has his own idea as to why the series was so popular. "It was very nice for people in the middle of an English winter to switch on the television to see lovely scenery, sunlit bays and all the rest of those things," he recalled.

"And what is nice about Jersey is that, even though it's only nine by five miles, it contains many locations. You might think you are in California if you are down at St Ouen's Beach with the sand dunes behind you and if you go to the north of the Island around Sorel Point you could think that you were in Cornwall, with the grey cliffs, small coves and great beaches."

"Therefore we could exploit that and we could get a camera crew around very quickly to very different locations. Most people who come across to the island are quite surprised to find out how small it is, because when we were filming we made it look much larger."

Sat nav references:

Forum cinema (JE2 4SU)

Haute de la Garenne (JE3 58P)

Mont Orgueil Castle (JE3 6ET)

The Old Court House (JE3 8AB)

St Ouen's Manor (JE3 2HR)

Ballykissangel

Avoca

Of course, the town of Avoca, in County Wicklow, which doubled on screen as the sleepy village of *Ballykissangel*, is actually in the Republic of Ireland and therefore obviously not part of Britain. It's included in this book simply because of the popularity of the BBC series and because it is within easy reach of the UK.

Above: (left) **Assumpta Fitzgerald (Dervla Kirwan) outside Fitzgerald's** *(centre)* **The bridge on Avoca** *(right)* **Father Peter Clifford (Stephen Tompkinson) in thoughtful mood** *Opposite page:* **Assumpta and Father Peter in a scene from the popular series.**

The series began in 1996 and ran until 2001 and saw rookie English priest Father Peter Clifford, played by Stephen Tompkinson, arrive to take on a new job as the local curate. He became friends with local bar owner Assumpta, played by Dervla Kirwan, and soon wised up to the ways of the locals.

He faced ongoing battles with his immediate superior, wily old priest Father MacAnally, played by Niall Toiban, and local businessman Brian Quigley, played by Tony Doyle. After two series both Stephen and Dervla decided to quit the show and two new characters Orla O'Connell, played by Victoria Smurfit and Sean Dillon, played by Lorcan Cranitch, were introduced to fill the gap and the series remained popular.

The real-life locals of Avoca were delighted with the success of the show and the influx of visitors it has brought them. Stephen Tompkinson was surprised by the number of tourists the show attracted to Avoca. "It was amazing," he recalled. "We had as many as 20 coachloads a day passing through when we were filming in the summer, plus all the people in cars, but they were all very good about letting us get on with it."

Most interior scenes for *Ballykissangel*, apart from Hendley's shop, which you can visit and has a fish and chip shop next door, are filmed in studios near Dublin but there's still plenty to see in Avoca. First stop might be Fitzgerald's, which plays Fitzgerald's on screen (the name was changed for filming and the owners decided to stick with it) and where you're bound to get a warm welcome. About 100 yards up the road is St Mary and St Patrick Church, which doubled as St Joseph's.

Then there is the local chemist which is used as the Post Office for filming. The locations for Quigley's House and Father Mac's are actually in Enniskerry, about 30 miles away. For more details see www. avoca.com and www.wicklow.ie

The Invisibles

Portaferry

Anyone heading to Devon in England to find the pretty seaside village which played home to semi-retired criminals Syd Woolsey and Maurice Riley in the 2008 BBC series *The Invisibles* will be wasting their time. That's because although the series, which starred Warren Clarke, Anthony Head, Jenny Agutter and Dean Lennox Kelly was set in the West Country, it was actually filmed in Portaferry in Northern Ireland which doubled as Bidmouth.

The Northern Ireland authorities and the Irish Republican government (where some other scenes were filmed) offer tax breaks to film and television producers so it was decided to film *The Invisibles* there. To make sure it looked like Devon set designers hid any obvious giveaway that it was in fact Northern Ireland and dressed the set with Devon miscellany like posters.

And in France

Merlin
The beautiful Château de Pierrefonds in northern France is obviously not in Britain but as the setting for the BBC's popular series *Merlin* we thought it was worth including. A castle has existed on the site since the 12th century and in addition to playing Camelot in *Merlin* it also appeared in the film *The Messenger: The Story of Joan of Arc*.

Monsignor Renard
Although the ITV drama *Monsignor Renard* also wasn't filmed in Britain, the location for it is included here because it is easy to reach. The late John Thaw starred in the four-part drama as a Catholic priest drawn into the French resistance while living in a town under Nazi occupation.

The drama was filmed in the beautiful town of Saint-Valery-sur-Somme which overlooks Somme Bay, famous as the site where William the Conqueror assembled his fleet before sailing over to England in 1066.

Acknowledgements

The authors are indebted to all those who helped with the preparation of this book especially: (alphabetically): Simon Allen, Heather Armitage, Ralph Assheton, Kevin Bell, Jenny Bradley, Rupert Bray, Richard Brown, Janet Bruton, Joseph Cairns, James Caterer, Nicola Cheriton-Sutton, Nicola Clark, Andrea Collitt, Rikke Dakin, Harvey Edgington, Thomas Elgood, Jenny Ellenger, Stephen Elliott, Claire Evans, Pat Eyre, Midge Ferguson, Fiona Frankham, John Friend Newman, Chris Fulcher, Robbie Gibbs, Tryphena Greenwood, Dee Gregson, Mark Grimwade, Paul Gulliver, Javis Gurr, Arron Hendy, David Hitchcock, Andi Hollingsworth, Kerry Ixer, Nicky James, Christina Joyce, Stacey Killon, Jamie Lengyel, Caroline Lowsley-Williams, Jamie Lovelace, Alice Lumley, Donald Mackinnon, Esther Mars, Nick Marshall, Richard May, Natalie Moore, Michael More-Molyneaux, Hayley Morgan, Jess Newbould, Catriona Newman, John Friend Newman, Karen Nicholson, Robert Noble, Adrian Notter, Michele Notter, Emily Ogden, Frances Pardell, Paul Pearson, Katherine Powley, Berenice Ray, Keith Righton, Theresa Robson, Helen Saunders, Keith Simmonds, Sandra Simmonds, Andrew Sharpe, Lady Angela Stucley, Tony Tarran, Gillian Thompson, Chris Tinsley, Sarah Upton, Paul Vigay, Jenni Wagstaffe, Pete Ware, Luc Webster, Rick Weston, Pam White, Gareth Williams, Brett Wilson and Stuart Wright.

Picture credits

The authors are also grateful to the photographers who kindly allowed their pictures to be used. They are credited below:

Jacket front: Cranford: David Betteridge www.dhbphotography.co.uk; Doc Martin: ITV/Rex Features; Midsomer Murders: © Bentley Productions; Downton Abbey: ITV/Rex Features; Doctor Who: Mark Campbell/Rex Features
Jacket rear: Downton Abbey: ITV / Rex Features; Only Fools and Horses: Radio Times.

Pages 2-3 www.dragon-pictures.com; page 9: Steve Clark; page 10: Kineta Hill; page 11: Martine van Meerbeeck; pages 11-14: David Betteridge www. dhbphotography.co.uk; pages 14 & 16: Steve Clark; page 15: Alan Davies www.bigaldavies.co.uk; page 17: Rex Features; page 18: David Betteridge www.dhbphotography.co.uk, pages 19 & 20: Chavenage; page 21: Steve Clark; page 22: Steve Clark • www.solentnews.biz • www.scopefeatures. com; pages 23 & 24: South West News Service (SWNS); page 24: Rick Weston; pages 25-26: Owen Benson www.owenbenson.co.uk; page 27: © English Heritage Photo Library; page 28: Lady Stucley; page 29: Loseley House; page 31: Mark Bourdillon / www.warnerleisurehotels.co.uk; page 32: ITV/Rex Features; pages 33 & 42: Kathy Cook; page 34, 36 & 37: ITV/Rex Features; page 35: Adrian Porter www.Ymzala.net; page 38: Caitlin Ferguson-Mir www. photoexpedition.co.uk; page 39: Eagle Eyes; page 40 & 41: ITV/Rex Features • Mark Emerson; pages 43-45 ITV / Rex Features; page 46: Rex Features • Mark Fanthorpe • Bob Mazzer www.bobmazzer.com; pages 47 & 48: Bob Mazzer • Justin Lycett / Hastings Observer; page 49: Rex Features; page 50: Tony Larkin/ Rex Features; page 51: Chester Tugwell; page 52: Tony Larkin/Rex Features; Midsomer Murders stills pages 53-55 © Bentley Productions; page 56: David Betteridge; page 57 © English Heritage Photo Library; page 58: Its Lefty • David Purton www.pictures4partners.co.uk / St Albans Register Office; page 59: Adrian Porter; page 60: The News, Portsmouth; page 61: Courtesy of the BBC; 62 & 63: Eagle Eyes; page 63: Steve Clark; page 64: Courtesy of the BBC; page 65: Dorset Echo; page 66: Royal Oak • Jamie Barras; page 68: Eagle Eyes; page 69: Jamie Barras; page 70: Terry Moran; page 71: Eagle Eyes; page 72: Lynford Hall Hotel • Edward Wing/Rex Features; page 73: Stuart Wright/ The Dad's Army Appreciation Society; pages 74 & 75; Nick Ford www.nickpix. co.uk; page 76: Eagle Eyes; page 77: Albanpix Ltd/Rex Features • Steve Clark; Page 78: © NTPL / Ray Hallett • Michael J Davis; Page 79 Harmitage; page 80: Rockingham Castle • www.shakespeare-country.co.uk; pages 81 & 82: Courtesy of www.britainonview.com; page 82: ITV/Rex Features; Page 84: Steve Poole / Scope Features; page 85 Kingpin Media; page 86: Minke Spiro/ Rex Features • Lincolnshire County Council; page 87: © Andrew Tryner / English Heritage Photo Library • ITV/Rex Features; pages 89-89: Charlie Morton; page 90: © NTPL / Rupert Truman; page 91: Mark Campbell/Rex Features; pages 92 & 93: www.dragon-pictures.com; pages: 94, 95, 96, 97 , 98, 100, 101, 102; www.walesnews.com; pages 97 and 99: page 102 (top): Rex Features; page 103: Rex Features • www.walesnews.com; page 104: The News, Portsmouth; page 105: Allan Ballard / www.scopefeatures.com; page 106: Darren Griffiths; page 107 & 108: www.portmeirion-village.com; page 108 & 109: Rex Features; page 110: www.llechwedd-slate-caverns.co.uk page 111: Mark Campbell/Rex Features; page 112: Liverpool Film Office • Steve Drewry; Page 113: ITV/Rex Features; Page 115 & 116: www.cavendish-press. co.uk; page 115 • Joseph Cairns; page 116: TVTimes/www.scopefeatures. com • © NTPL / Matthew Antrobus; page 117: Nick Fletcher; page 118: Rex Features • Ribble Valley Borough Council; page 119: Mike Kipling www. mikekipling.com; pages 120 & 121: Karen Lewis; page 121: Tim Green; page 1122-123: Keith Simmonds www.glendalehouse.co.uk; page 124: © NTPL / Andrew Butler; page 125: © NTPL / Joe Cornish; page 126: Kirklees Council • Joyce Turner; page 127: Rex Features; page 128: Helen Ibbotson • Richard Brown; page 129: Mark Dyson; page 130: Newcastle City Council; page 131: Paul Beentjes; page132 Barbara Jones; pages 133 & 134: www.visitscotland. com; page 135: Brian Moody / Scope Features; page 136: www.scopefeatures. com; pages137, 138 &139: www.jersey.com; page 138: Chris Craymer / www. scopefeatures.com; page 140: World Productions Ltd / BBC Photo Library • Chris Hill / www.discoverireland.com; page 141: World Productions Ltd / BBC Photo Library • Steve Clark

Selected references & useful further reading

Bergerac's Jersey by John Nettles (BBC Books, 1988), The Bill - The Inside Story of British Television's Most Successful Police Series by Tony Lynch (Boxtree, 1991), Doctor Who magazine, The Only Fools and Horses Story by Steve Clark (BBC Books, 1998), Only Fools and Horses - The Official Inside Story by Steve Clark (Splendid Books, 2011), The World of Inspector Morse by Christopher Bird (Boxtree, 1998), The World of Jonathan Creek by Steve Clark (BBC Books, 1999) and www.doctorwholocations.net

The authors would be pleased to hear from readers with details of new locations and updates on existing ones. Please contact them at locationguide@ splendidbooks.co.uk or via the address on page 6.

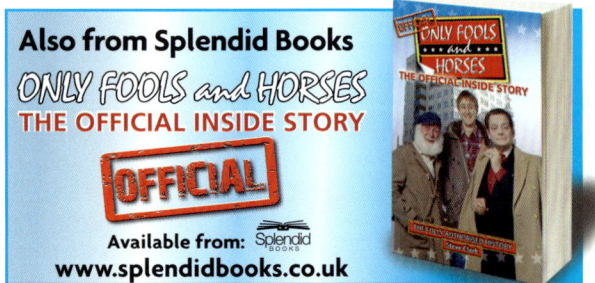

Also from Splendid Books
ONLY FOOLS and HORSES
THE OFFICIAL INSIDE STORY
OFFICIAL
Available from: Splendid Books
www.splendidbooks.co.uk

Index